Kuala Lumpur, Malaysia

Travel and Tourism

Author
Caleb Gray.

SONITTEC PUBLISHING. All rights reserved. No part of this publication may be reproduced, distributed, or transmitted in any form or by any means, including photocopying, recording, or other electronic or mechanical methods, without the prior written permission of the publisher, except in the case of brief quotations embodied in critical reviews and certain other noncommercial uses permitted by copyright law. For permission requests, write to the publisher, addressed "Attention: Permissions Coordinator," at the address below.

Copyright © 2019 Sonittec Publishing
All Rights Reserved

First Printed: 2019.

Publisher:
SONITTEC LTD
College House, 2nd
Floor
17 King Edwards
Road,
Ruislip
London
HA4 7AE

Table of Content

SUMMARY 1
INTRODUCTION 5
HISTORY 7
TOURISM 15
   QUICK GUIDE TO KUALA LUMPUR 15
      Sightseeing in Kuala 15
      Family trip with kids 19
      Cuisine & restaurants 23
      Traditions & lifestyle 25
      Culture: sights to visit 28
      Attractions & nightlife 30
      Tips for tourists 32
   MAIN ATTRACTIONS 35
      Aquaria KLCC in Kuala Lumpur 36
      ASEAN Sculpture Garden 40
      Badan Warisan Malaysia in Kuala Lumpur 42
      Batu Caves in Kuala Lumpur 45
         Thaipusam in Batu Caves 48
      Berjaya Times Square Theme Park 52
      Blue Coral Aquarium at KL Tower 54
      Blue Mosque Selangor 56
      Kuala Lumpur Little India Brickfields 57
      Buddhist Maha Vihara Temple 61
      KLCC - Bukit Bintang Walkway in KL 63
      Bukit Jalil National Sports Complex Malaysia 65
      Bukit Jalil Golf & Country Resort KL 67
      Bukit Unggul Country Club 68
      Cathedral of St. Mary in Kuala Lumpur 70
      Central Market Kuala Lumpur 71
      Chan See Shu Yuen Temple in Kuala Lumpur 75
      Chow Kit Market in Kuala Lumpur 77
      Dayabumi Complex Kuala Lumpur 79
      District 21 Kuala Lumpur 80

Firefly Watching & Kuala Selangor Kampung Tour 83
Genting Highlands Park 85
Holy Rosary Church Kuala Lumpur 89
i-City in Shah Alam 91
Iron Mosque Putrajaya 95
Istana Budaya in Kuala Lumpur 96
Istana Negara in Kuala Lumpur 100
Kidzania Kuala Lumpur 104
KLCC Park in Kuala Lumpur 107
KL Forest Eco Park (formerly Bukit Nanas Forest 109
Kuala Lumpur Butterfly Park in Lake Gardens 110
Kuala Lumpur City Gallery 112
Kuala Lumpur Convention Centre 114
Kuala Lumpur Upside Down House at KL Tower 116
Kuan Ti Temple in Kuala Lumpur 118
Kuan Yin Temple in Kuala Lumpur 120
Tun Abduk Razak Heritage Park 122
Lake Gardens Kuala Lumpur Segway Tour 125
Madras Lane Petaling Street 127
Masjid Jamek Mosque 129
Masjid Negara Mosque in Kuala Lumpur 131
Masjid Raja Fisabilillah Cyberjaya 133
Megakidz Funland & Edutainment at Mid Valley 135
Merdeka Square in Kuala Lumpur 138
Menara KL Tower 140
Movie Animation Park Studios Malaysia 142
Islamic Arts Museum Malaysia 145
National Monument in Kuala Lumpur 148
National Museum in Kuala Lumpur 151
National Planetarium in Kuala Lumpur 154
National Science Centre in Kuala Lumpur 156
National Textiles Museum Kuala Lumpur 157
National Visual Arts Gallery in Kuala Lumpur 161
Kuala Lumpur Zoo, Pandas & Aquarium 164
Perdana Botanical Garden in Kuala Lumpur 167

Petronas Art Gallery in Kuala Lumpur........................... 170
Petronas Twin Towers in Kuala Lumpur........................ 171
Petrosains in Kuala Lumpur... 175
Putra World Trade Centre in Kuala Lumpur 179
Royal Malaysian Police Museum 181
Royal Selangor Visitor's Centre 184
Rumah Penghulu Abu Seman...................................... 188
Sky Box at Sky Deck KL Tower 191
Sri Kandaswamy Kovil Hindu Temple........................... 192

NIGHTLIFE.. 194
Changkat Bukit Bintang Nightlife................................. 196
Great Rooftop Bars in KL... 204
   Marini's on 57 Kuala Lumpur 204
   SkyBar at Traders Hotels in KL...207
   Luna Bar in Pacific Regency Suites....................................210
Troika Sky Dining at Kuala Lumpur 213
Chinatown Kuala Lumpur Nightlife.............................. 216
   PS150 Bar Kuala Lumpur..218
   Reggae Bar Chinatown in Kuala Lumpur 220

SHOPPING... 222
Bukit Bintang Shopping... 223
   Pavilion Shopping Mall in Kuala Lumpur 224
   Starhill Gallery Kuala Lumpur..230
   Low Yat Plaza Shopping Mall...235
Kuala Lumpur Chinatown Shopping............................ 239
   Kasturi Walk in Kuala Lumpur 240
   Petaling Street in Chinatown...242

HOTELS 247

Kuala Lumpur, Malaysia

Summary

The importance of travelling in our life?

Everyone has their very own reasons to travel. Some people travel for work, some travel for pleasure while for others it is just a way of life. They travel to live and to escape at the same time.

Whatever might be the reason to travel, here are few ways in which travelling would definitely change you and I think that is why travelling becomes so important in life:

<u>Enjoy being alone</u>: There is something therapeutic about being alone and being at peace with it. While you soak in a new culture, you also connect with your own inner self.

<u>Learn to adapt</u>**:** It is a different world out there, literally. Be it the pace of life, the language or simply the change in weather, it is always a change and you have to adapt to it. This is what makes travelling truly beautiful as you break away from the routine and adapt to something totally new.

<u>Experience a new culture</u>: Every place comes with its distinct cultural habits, you cannot think about New York without talking about its fast paced life and about Italy without enjoying its relaxed lifestyle. Similarly, while visiting the UK you might have to be a bit formal in your interactions with the locals, on the other hand, while greeting the people in Thailand, one can be really warm and casual.

<u>Broaden your taste buds</u>: Travelling without experiencing the local food is just not complete. It is not only a culinary experience but a cultural one as well.

Kuala Lumpur, Malaysia

<u>Get out of comfort zone</u>: From simple experiences like the weather, way of life or food to the more adventurous ones like trying a new sport, travelling really pushes ones boundaries to the core. You might end up participating in a street carnival in Brazil just like the locals or trying the local delicacies (read insects) in Thailand.

<u>Indulge in Photography</u>: It does not matter whether you are a professional or not. It is also irrelevant whether you have a DSLR or a very basic camera, while travelling what matters is the love and quest for seeing beautiful places and the sheer joy of capturing them in your lense. Travelling would in return give you your very own collection of amazing postcards of beautiful sunsets, snow laced mountains or sunny beaches.

<u>Learn to escape</u>: Travelling is the best way to break the routine. If you are in a bustling city, go ahead and experience the country life. If you are in a rural place, travel to a bustling city and experience its madness.

Stressed with the city life or work pressure? A spa break in Himalayas or Kerala is a must try.

Appreciate Nature: The quest to explore more when one is travelling always leads to a sense of amazement about nature. While most of us keep a track of technological advancements, Nature has its own ways of outshining all of these. The Antelope Canyon in Arizona or Turquoise Ice in Russia are the finest examples of this. For more, check out the most unbelievable places around the world.

Get closer to your own roots: While one travels and experiences a lot of different cultures and practices, it definitely brings one closer to his or her own roots. Travel helps one appreciate one's identity and culture.

Travelling is all about experiences. They can happen in terms of culture, people, places but most importantly with one's own self and this was all about

Introduction

Kuala Lumpur, capital of Malaysia. The city is located in west-central Peninsular (West) Malaysia, midway along the west coast tin and rubber belt and about 25 miles (40 km) east of its ocean port, Port Kelang, on the Strait of Malacca. It is the country's largest urban area and its cultural, commercial, and transportation centre. In 1972 Kuala Lumpur was designated a municipality, and in 1974 this entity and adjacent portions of surrounding Selangor state became a federal territory.

Kuala Lumpur lies in hilly country astride the confluence of the Kelang and Gombak rivers; its name in Malay means "muddy estuary." Malaysia's Main Range rises nearby to the north, east, and southeast. The climate is equatorial, with high temperatures and humidity that vary little throughout the year. The area receives about 95 inches (2,400 mm) of rain annually; June and July are the driest months. Area federal territory, 94 square miles (243 square km). Pop. (2009 est.) city, 1,493,000; (2010) federal territory, 1,674,621.

Kuala Lumpur, Malaysia

History

The origin of Kuala Lumpur dates to 1857, when a group of 87 Chinese tin miners founded a settlement at what is now the suburb of Ampang. Strategically commanding both river valleys, the community flourished as a tin-collecting centre despite its malaria-infested jungle location. In 1880 Kuala Lumpur superseded Klang (now Kelang) as the state capital, and its rapid growth thereafter has been attributed to Sir Frank Swettenham, British resident after 1882. He initiated construction on the Klang–Kuala Lumpur Railway and encouraged the use of brick and tile in buildings as a precaution against fire and as an aid to better health. The city's central position led to its choice as capital of the Federated Malay States (1895).

The city was occupied by the Japanese (1942–45) in World War II. Its population greatly increased in the postwar years during a long (1948–60) communist-led guerrilla insurgency, and under a resettlement program new villages were established on the city's outskirts. Kuala Lumpur became the capital of the independent Federation of Malaya in 1957 and of Malaysia in 1963. Growth continued, spurred by industrial development; the population reached a half million in the mid-1960s and passed one million in the early 1980s. Population growth brought increased congestion, however, which, with Malaysian government offices scattered across the city, hampered administration. Consequently, many of the federal offices were moved to the new city of Putrajaya, about 15 miles (25 km) south of Kuala Lumpur, about the turn of the 21st century. Putrajaya subsequently became the country's administrative centre, while Kuala Lumpur remained the capital.

The Contemporary City

Kuala Lumpur, Malaysia

The city comprises a mixture of modern and traditional architecture; such structures as glass-and-concrete skyscrapers, elegant mosques, Chinese shop-houses (family-operated shops with the business on the ground floor and the family's living space upstairs), squatters' huts, and Malay stilt *kampung*s ("villages") betray Western, Middle Eastern, East Asian, and local influences. While its centre along the embanked Kelang is heavily congested, its municipal area and suburbs are well planned. The commercial quarter, called the Golden Triangle, is concentrated on the river's east side. Among its sleek high-rise buildings are two of the world's tallest buildings: the 1,483-foot (452-metre) Petronas Twin Towers, designed by Argentine-American architect Cesar Pelli; and one of the tallest broadcasting and telecommunications masts, the 1,381-foot (421-metre) Kuala Lumpur Tower. Government buildings and the notable railway station (all influenced by Moorish design) are on the river's hilly west bank. This nucleus is surrounded by a zone of Chinese two-story wooden shop-houses and mixed residential areas of Malay *kampung*s, modern bungalows, and middle-income brick flats. The exclusive Bukit Tunku (or Kenny Hills) sector is a showcase for upscale dwellings and other structures that blend multiple architectural styles.

Malays, who are Muslim, are the city's largest ethnic group. Despite the prevalence of domes and minarets associated with Islamic architecture, however, the non-Muslim Chinese dominate the city and its economy. The mostly Hindu Indian minority, connected historically with nearby rubber estates, also is substantial. Many Malays are employed in government service, and Kampung Baru is one of the city's few concentrated Malay residential sections.

The industrial suburb of Sungai Besi ("Iron River") has iron foundries and engineering works and factories that process food and soap. The Sentul and Ipoh Road area is the site of railway (assembly and construction) and engineering workshops and sawmills, and cement is manufactured at Rawang to the north. While Kuala

Lumpur has diversified manufacturing, the focus of industrial planning is in the adjacent suburbs of Petaling Jaya and Batu Tiga, notably in the high-technology sector. Kuala Lumpur is the country's centre of banking and finance; activities related to these and other services, including tourism, have become increasingly important. The local Batu Arang coalfield and the Connaught Bridge thermal electric power station near Kelang are the main sources, respectively, of the city's fuel supply and power.

Kuala Lumpur, with its central position in Peninsular Malaysia, is the hub of the peninsula's transportation system, and rail lines and major roads radiate from it. Air service is largely through Kuala Lumpur International Airport, located about 30 miles (50 km) south at Sepang. The city itself has an extensive network of multilane roads and express highways, although these are inadequate for the growing number of cars and trucks. A light-rail public transit system—inaugurated in 1996 and now consisting of three interconnected lines—has eased traffic congestion somewhat.

There are several hospitals and state clinics, including a modern tuberculosis centre and the well-equipped Institute of Medical Research (1900). The Rubber Research Institute (1925) and Radio and Television Malaysia are headquartered there. The University of Malaya was founded at Kuala Lumpur in 1962. Tunku Abdul Rahman College was established there in 1969, followed by the International Islamic University Malaysia in 1983. In addition, the Malay-language National University of Malaysia opened in Kuala Lumpur in 1970; the main campus is now in nearby Bangi, but there is still a branch in the city.

Lake Gardens, extending westward from the Kelang River opposite the central city, is an extensive greenbelt containing orchid and other gardens, wildlife areas, the government's Parliament House, the National Museum of Malaysia (1963), the Islamic Arts Museum Malaysia (1999), and the National

Planetarium (1993). A smaller natural area, Bukit Nanas ("Pineapple Hill") Forest Reserve, is just northwest of the Golden Triangle. Nearby are the National Art Gallery (1958), the National Library of Malaysia (1966), and the National Theatre.

Notable civic buildings include the Moorish-style Sultan Abdul Samad Building (formerly the Secretariat Building), the more contemporary National Mosque (Masjid Negara), and the old Sultan's Mosque (Masjid Jame), which is on a peninsula at the junction of the Kelang and Gombak rivers in the city centre. Just south of the city is the National Sports Complex, constructed for the 1998 Commonwealth Games; among its several sports venues is the 100,000-seat National Stadium. A short distance to the east is the National Zoo and Aquarium. At the northern edge of the federal territory is Batu ("Rock") Caves, a complex of limestone grottoes including a 400-foot- (122-metre-) high outcropping reached by hundreds of steps that contains a Hindu temple and is the scene of an elaborate festival,

Thaipusam, in honour of the Hindu deity Subramaniam (or Skanda). A short distance north of the caves is Templer Park, a jungle preserve.

Tourism
Quick Guide to Kuala Lumpur
Sightseeing in Kuala

Lumpur what to see. Complete travel guide

Kuala Lumpur is a city in Malaysia that is located on the south-east of Malay Peninsula in a beautiful valley surrounded by mountains. Kuala Lumpur is an ultramodern megalopolis, a large Asian industrial and cultural center that has got its modern look within just 10 years. The city organically combines technologies of Western countries and mysterious East.

Kuala Lumpur features tropical climate. The average yearly temperature of air here estimates +27C with relative humidity of 96%. It rains often in Kuala Lumpur.

If someone thinks the city looks more like a desert, he/she is wrong. Kuala Lumpur simply dives in greenery. Around twenty years ago best landscape designers have created projects of several green parks that have been laid out on banks of the picturesque lake. Today Garden of Orchids, Garden of Butterflies, Garden of Birds, and Garden of Deer are popular city's destinations for rest. In the Garden of Deer you can see a rare animal mouse deer. It is approximately as big as a cat and lives exclusively in this part of South-East of Asia.

Another sight of Kuala Lumpur is Petronas Twin Towers - the tallest building in the world that is famous by its size and complexity of project. The look of the building has distinct Islamic traits. The complex consists of two towers that are connected by a bridge. The bridge is a wonderful observation area featuring stunning looks of the city. You can also visit Menara tower (421 meter high), Chinatown a famous trading region, a national mosque Masjid Negara, historical architectural buildings City's Council, Department of Information, Main Post Office, Sultan Abdul Samad Palace (nowadays Supreme Soviet), Dataran Merdeka and much more.

The most interesting sites are the caves of Batu ancient limestone caves, in which hundreds of years ago were temples. Next to these caves is one of the largest Buddha statues in the world. In these, places every year, the Festival of Thaipusam, which attracts a huge number of pilgrims, is held. The caves themselves are an outstanding natural attraction. They were formed more than 400 million years ago.

One of the most beautiful architectural monuments of the city is the royal palace. It was built in 1928 by one of the wealthy Chinese millionaires and until 1957, was privately owned. Subsequently, the building was bought by the government. It still remains the current residence of the monarch of Malaysia. The vast adjoining territory of the garden is decorated with landscape compositions. Many tourists come here to look at the guard, who is dressed in a luxurious form. A popular observation of tourists is the watching of the changing of the guard.

In Kuala-Lumpur, there is a magnificent botanical garden. It contains the rarest species of plants from around the world. The territory of the park is divided into several thematic zones, where you can admire not only exotic plants, but also amazing fauna. There are several museums and monuments on the territory of the park, and there is also a planetarium, which will be interesting to visit by the whole family.

One of the oldest buildings in the city is the Jamek Mosque. Absolutely everyone can visit this incredibly beautiful mosque and admire its interior decoration, regardless of religion. This mosque was eventually completed in 1909. Many elements of its internal and external design were preserved in their original form.

There are many interesting museums in the city; among them is the Museum of Asian Art. In addition to traditional paintings and sculptures, there is a very interesting collection of ceramics. The age of many exhibits here is more than 200 years. The most multifaceted and extensive exhibit is the collection of the National Museum. Here you can see a variety of items of folk crafts, works of art, collections of old coins and weapons. The museum has a large collection of natural science exhibits. It will be interesting to visit with childre

Family trip with kids

Family trip to Kuala Lumpur with children. Ideas on where to go with your child
In Kuala Lumpur, the choice of entertainment for vacationers with children is simply unbelievable. The entertainment center Berjaya Time Square Theme Park enjoys great popularity among tourists with children. It is located on the territory of a large shopping complex. In this amusement park, a wide selection of colorful attractions is equipped, including the popular "roller coaster". Various game simulators are prepared for

children. Visitors of the center can diversify the recreation by walking in shops and relaxing in local cafes.

The magnificent Desa Water Park is located in the city. This water park is outdoors and occupies a rather large territory. It includes a beautiful pool with artificial waves, special pools for young children, colorful slides of varying difficulty, and next to the pool, spacious terraces for sunbathing. Since the water park is very large, there are never any queues in it even on a day off. You can relax here in a pleasant uncrowded environment.

There are many original entertainment centers in the city. With older children, you can go to the Flight Experience Center Kuala Lumpur. It offers visitors the opportunity to try out the latest state-of-the-art games, which simulates a flight on a plane with maximum accuracy. Here, under the guidance of an experienced instructor, you can learn how to lift an "airplane" into the sky, control it, and land. Both adults and children will get a lot of impressions from such entertainment.

There are many cafes and restaurants in Kuala Lumpur that are suitable for families, but there are some special ones, among them, the Boarders Tabletop Games Café. This is an original cafe in which it is possible not only to try famous dishes, but also to play various table games. Large companies of youth, and families with children often come to the café to relax. Besides the classical halls, there is a special hall for games here, with comfortable tables and chairs. A more original place than this to relax in the height of a hot afternoon will be difficult to find.

Children should definitely visit the Aquaria KLCC. It has a well put together design and is one of the largest oceanarium in the world. The aquarium has a large transparent tunnel. During a walk along the tunnel, you can feel yourself as part of the amazing underwater world. Large sharks, stingrays, as well as hundreds of exotic fish of various colors live in large aquariums here. The aquarium is decorated with original thematic installations, against which you can make original photographs.

In the popular Malaysian resort, there is a great zoo - KL Tower Mini Zoo. It is quite small, but guarantees a mass of impressions to its visitors. Colorful parrots, miniature monkeys, meerkats, iguanas and turtles, as well as cute rabbits which all children love, live in the zoo. Visitors are allowed to pat and feed many inhabitants to the zoo. This mini zoo will be interesting to visit even with young children.

Another original place suitable for exploring nature is Kuala Lumpur Butterfly Park. The main inhabitants of this picturesque park are butterflies, and they can be seen in dozens of different species. In the park, interesting excursions are organized, during which visitors are told a lot of interesting information about the most beautiful insects of the planet. On the territory of the park, there is a small museum in which a collection of insects from different parts of the world is represented. This is only but a small part of the unusual attractions that you can visit with children in Kuala Lumpur.

Cuisine & restaurants

Cuisine of Kuala Lumpur for gourmets. Places for dinner best restaurants

Local cuisine can be called one of the most diverse in the world. Culinary traditions represent a unique combination of Indian, Chinese, Malaysian and African features. Even a great connoisseur would get lost in a variety of national dishes. Everywhere you can taste the traditional curry and chicken, delicious fish and noodles. The most important feedstuff is rice; it is the basis of most national dishes. Rice can be fried with vegetables and spices, steamed or mixed with pieces of fruit for desserts, stewed in coconut milk and served as excellent side dishes.

In national cuisine restaurant guests would be offered rice with vegetables or seafood, it can be complemented with a wide variety of components. In addition to diverse restaurants, you can find a huge number of outdoor stalls in the city, which sell a wide variety of delicacies. Many of such eating places may seem questionable, but they are very popular among the indigenous population. Dishes are always fresh and tasty, so some of the stalls are no less popular than well-known restaurants.

In the mid-day long queues can line up to them - so large the number of regular customers is. Usually stalls offer a decent portion of rice with an addition that customer picks for himself. Selection of additional components is usually great: fresh and steamed vegetables, fish and exotic seafood, as well as all satay ayam kebabs of meat or chicken. These stalls also differ with reasonable prices, which would come in handy for budget travelers.

The most important meal is breakfast; in the morning, the menu of restaurants and cafes strikes by diversity. The most popular dish for breakfast among the indigenous people is nasi lemak. It is rice cooked in coconut milk that is complemented with boiled eggs, anchovies, cucumber and roasted peanuts. Despite the abundance of components, their combination is very successful. Some restaurants offer traditional Chinese dishes. Peking duck here is just as good as seafood and rice. In Kuala Lumpur vegetarian restaurants are common. You can also find a lot of interesting delicacies in their menus.

Traditions & lifestyle

Colors of Kuala Lumpur traditions, festivals, mentality and lifestyle

Kuala Lumpur is a cosmopolitan city; its culture is interesting and many-sided. During the year, locals celebrate a lot of interesting festivals, which include both European and Muslim, Buddhist and Hindu celebrations. Among European holidays the most prominent are colorful New Year and Christian Easter. However, supporters of Muslim ignore those holidays; the most important event for them is celebration of

Prophet Muhammad's birthday. On this day Koran is read in all mosques. There are no noisy and colorful celebration activities. It is customary to celebrate it within family circle and spend the day in prayer.

For travelers the most interesting are Buddhist holidays, which are real leaders in beauty and originality of events. An interesting event is the Moon Cake Festival; many interesting stories and legends are associated with it.

According to one of them, during the war with Mongols, locals passed secret messages to each other in cakes. Little notes were wrapped in dough; flatbreads served as reliable protection from prying eyes. Since then, every year locals bake smart round cakes, which are very similar to the full moon, and treat their loved ones.

No less interesting is the origin of the Lantern Festival. According to an old legend, the fearsome dragon has decided to deprive the light from the people. Upon learning of his plans, residents have made a lot of lanterns and, when darkness came, moved with them to streets. Dragon wasn't able to select which lantern to start with, and died of vexation. A good tradition to make colorful lanterns has kept for many centuries. There are always solemn parades and entertainment in Kuala Lumpur in this festive day. It ends with a large-scale festival procession in which each participant has to pick the lantern with him.

In September capital welcomes the Festival of Malaysia, which is considered the longest-running and most colorful holiday. It usually takes at least two weeks; residents from all the states of the country participate in the celebration. The festival includes a variety of events, from concerts and traditional children performances to the exciting culinary and sports competitions. No less interesting is the Flower festival, which usually takes place in July. For several days, the city turns into a huge fragrant garden

Culture: sights to visit

Culture of Kuala Lumpur. Places to visit old town, temples, theaters, museums and palaces

Colonial part of the city would be most attractive for travelers, as main historical and architectural landmarks are concentrated here. Here is a beautiful mosque Masjid Jamek, the construction of which took place in the early 20th century. The prototype of this beautiful architectural structure is the Mongolian mosque located in northern India. No less interesting is Sultan Abdul Samad, the State Secretariat. It is a beautiful building with domes and high tower that is a prime example of Moorish architecture.

Nearby is the Textile Museum; there you can see a fine collection, which will be interesting for everyone. In addition to original textile, museum's collection includes products from beads, hand embroidery and rosaries, as well as a lot of other beautiful handicrafts. An old English cathedral, St Mary's Church, is also situated in historic district. It had been founded in 1984, one hundred years later a large-scale reconstruction of the church had begun, and in 1989 part of the old building has been converted into a museum. It would be appreciated by numismatists as the museum is dedicated to old Malaysian money.

For those who want to get acquainted with the history of the country an excursion to the Museum of National History is dedicated. In addition to the permanent exhibition of historical artifacts, there are often collections of exhibits dedicated to various topics in it. The museum has become a permanent venue for all kinds of exhibitions and demonstrations. The largest collection of paintings in the country is represented in the Art Gallery. Among exhibits are paintings of both local and foreign artists.

The most important religious landmark of the whole country is the Masjid Negara mosque. Its construction was finally completed only in 1965. The main decoration of the mosque is a large-scale 18-end dome in the shape of a star. The main hall of the mosque is free to accommodate 8,000 pilgrims; the minaret is 73 meters height. Among monuments of modern architecture, Dayabumi Complex building is notable. A beautiful 35-story skyscraper located on the Raya street is home to office buildings, as well as the popular shopping center. No less attractive is Chinatown district, where unusual architectural buildings, museums and interesting shops are represented.

Attractions & nightlife

City break in Kuala Lumpur. Active leisure ideas for Kuala Lumpur attractions, recreation and nightlife

One of the favorite pastimes of the tourists is shopping and strolling around markets, but in addition to the attractive shopping centers, some other interesting entertainment could be discovered in almost every area. One of the busiest districts of the capital is the Jalan Bukit Bintang, there are more than ten largest shopping and entertainment complexes. Among these centers, Kuala Lumpur Plaza, Lot 10, Imbi Plaza and Starhill point out. In all of them there is a wide variety of shops, attractive restaurants and cafes.

The Sogo center is perfect for a family rest; this center is located in a beautiful tower-block. In addition to the popular stores, several playgrounds, excellent leisure centers for children and recreation areas for adults are open here. There are also several large supermarkets in Sogo, where you can buy any delicacies; there are also attractive clothing stores and even antique shops. It would take more than one day to explore all shopping center pavilions.

Central market attracts not only fans of shopping, but also gourmets. That's because of several popular restaurants and cafes serving in this area. Those, who want to enjoy local delicacies, have to look into one of these gastronomic places. Many shopping complexes work exclusively at night; the Chow Kit Market begins serving visitors in the evening. Here visitors are offered to buy excellent leather, local textiles, crafts and beautiful tin utensils.

The best place to explore is Chinatown; this area is considered one of the most beautiful in the city. Here you can spend hours strolling through the picturesque streets, admiring beautiful public gardens and squares. Travelers are also attracted by jewelry stores located here, where you can find a truly unique product. Fans of outdoor activities are recommended to go for a walk around the Lake Gardens Park located on a high hill. There is also a planetarium there; visit to it would enliven vacations and make it even more unique. In the planetarium scientific films are broadcasted. Fun shows, exhibitions and original excursions are often held there.

Tips for tourists

Preparing your trip to Kuala Lumpur: advices & hints things to do and to obey

1. There are no strict rules regarding dress here; locals hold an informal style, they can even visit important activities in casual clothes. For exploring the city casual wear is perfect, here it is prevalent among people of all ages.

2. Going for a walk, be sure to have sunscreen with you, as sun is particularly crafty in summer months. For those, who expect to spend time outdoors, repellents would be useful.

3. It is uncommon to leave a tip in restaurants and hotels. In some upscale places, it may be included in the bill and is usually not more than 10% of the total order.

4. Locals are very hospitable, so in any case don't refuse an invitation to come for a visit. Welcoming hosts would obviously offer guests some drinks and food that won't be refused too.

5. It's common to greet each other with a limp handshake. Hugs are suitable only for close friends or relatives; during intercourse no touching is allowed.

6. You have to take and pass food, money and other items with your right hand only. If you pass an object with your left hand, then this would be considered a serious insult, and may cause resentment.

7. On entering the religious objects and living spaces be sure to take off your shoes. Travelers who expect to attend mosques and other places of worship should choose clothes carefully. It shouldn't be too bright and open-necked.

8. It's worth to go to local markets with enough notes of small face value. In such way it would be easier to settle with sellers. You can pay with a credit card can in major supermarkets and upmarket shops.

9. Be sure to bargain on markets and in private trading pavilions. Even if you haven't succeeded in lowering price, you can reckon on a nice souvenir from the

seller. It is also worth to mention that some markets work exclusively at night.

10. Hand language is rather peculiar and has a ton of features. For example, during a conversation in any case don't point off any object or person with your forefinger, as this gesture is offensive. Don't touch the head, which is consider sacred by locals. Stroking a head is prohibited, children are no exception

Main Attractions

Kuala Lumpur attractions are very extensive and diverse, and as Malaysia's capital, that's hardly surprising. This city can be overwhelming for first-time visitors and with so much to see and do, not to mention a constantly evolving landscape, you're sure to miss out on some great sights unless you're well informed. That being said, we've compiled these attractions below in alphabetical order, so you can easily make the most out of your trip in Kuala Lumpur.

There are attractions in Kuala Lumpur to suit all ages, ranging from century-old landmarks, towering urban architecture, as well as sprawling gardens and animal parks. If you're interested in learning about the city's rich heritage, there are plenty of temples, museums, atmospheric Chinese architecture, and grand buildings with Moorish, Mogul and Malay architecture. Alternatively, the city's nightlife attractions are most easily accessible within the Golden Triangle area, and if it's nature you're after then the Lake Gardens and KLCC Park are perfect for those leisurely afternoons.

Aquaria KLCC in Kuala Lumpur

Aquaria KLCC, located on the concourse level of the Kuala Lumpur Convention Centre, is said to be one of the largest aquariums in Southeast Asia. Home to over 150 species of marine life, its star attractions include scary tiger sharks, lethal sea snakes, blue rays, bright coral fish, seahorses and more.

Kuala Lumpur, Malaysia

It's a well-stocked aquarium just begging to be explored, and after a few hours here you'll have seen over 5,000 freshwater and marine creatures, including massive arapaimas, giant groupers, gar fish and more. Some people write it off as a tourist trap, but they're sorely missing out beyond the big tanks, with gallons of water, filled with necklaces of kelp, coral and mysterious and sometimes menacing sea creatures, is one of the country's foremost sightseeing attractions with real depth and complexity.

Well worth exploring, Kuala Lumpur Aquarium doesn't just 'submerge' visitors beneath thousands of gallons of seawater instead the venue is laid out to take visitors through different watery landscapes, from the highlands and flooded jungles of Malaysia, to the Amazon basin, coral reefs and the open ocean. Your journey isn't a linear one start off on Level 1 where you'll see piranhas make quick work of their meal as well as electric eels, elephantnose fish and electric catfish. Also in this section, visitors can check out the

DNA Touch Pool where they can pick up and feel the texture of live corals and star fish.

The Tunnel at Aquaria KLCC

One of the highlights of Aquaria KLCC is a giant tank (featuring an authentic-looking shipwreck) a 90m walk-through tunnel with a moving travelator in its centre. Inside you'll be surrounded by sand tiger sharks, huge stingrays and more. You can take a break from looking at Nemo and his crew, as you head to The Stream which plays host to the giant water rat and the adorable Asian small-clawed otter. Meanwhile, the Jewels of the Jungle section is home to a variety of reptiles, amphibians and insects including the green snake, coatimundi, tarantula and many others; also be sure to check out the exhibit showcasing the life cycle of butterflies.

Weird and Wonderful

Level 2 sees you journeying through the Amazon Flooded Forest where the oversized araipaima, red tail catfish and many others dwell; next, head up to The

Coast to see archer fish, horseshoe crabs and more. Later, develop a deep appreciation for deep sea inhabitants such as the octopus and giant blotched fantail ray at the Oceanarium. Lastly, the Weird & Wonderful section is home to chambered nauticus, sea jelly and more, while the Coral Discovery Section has the requisite array of coral, seahorses and more. What's more, catch the fish feeding sessions which take place on Mondays, Wednesdays and Saturdays in the 2.5 million-litre aquarium.

Diving with Sharks

The best parts of Aquaria KLCC might actually be when you're feeling a little lost either literally, given the sheer size of this place, or figuratively, as you try to learn as much as you can about the oftentimes ignored multifaceted deep sea world. Though the aquaria revels in simple pleasures, thrill seekers are also well catered for they can get-up-close-and-personal with tiger sharks, stingrays and more as the aquarium has a Diving with Sharks program. Even though visitors have to sign a liability waiver form in order to strap on tanks, it's a safe environment as the sharks have been in Aquaria KLCC for more than five years now and are domesticated. Those who don't have diving permits can join the Cage Rage programme where visitors take the plunge into the tank within the confines of a submerged cage.

While this elegant underwater world may seem a kid-centric attraction, it caters well to all ages. There are plenty of reasons to 'dive in' and those who do will not regret it. After all, how many people can say they explored oceans in just a few hours?

Aquaria KLCC
Opening Hours: Daily 10:00 - 20:00
MRT: KLCC
Address: Kuala Lumpur Convention Centre Complex, Kuala Lumpur City Centre
Tel: +603 2333 1888

ASEAN Sculpture Garden

Kuala Lumpur, Malaysia

ASEAN Sculpture Garden was established in 1987 in commemoration of the 20th anniversary of the Association of Southeast Asian Nations (ASEAN). Located within Tun Abdul Razak Heritage Park, it contains a variety of public art installations by renowned artists from Singapore, Malaysia, the Philippines, Thailand, Indonesia and Brunei.

These sculptures are made from materials such as wood, glass, steel, marble, iron and bamboo, with detailed descriptions for each artwork in English and Malay. Perfect for those looking to enjoy some peace and quiet in KL City Centre, ASEAN Sculpture Garden is less crowded than other areas in Lake Gardens Kuala Lumpur.

Getting To and Around ASEAN Sculpture Garden

Due to its compact size, exploring the entirety of ASEAN Sculpture Garden takes less than 30 minutes, so we highly recommend walking to Tun Abdul Razak Heritage Park's other landmarks such as the National

Monument, Perdana Botanical Gardens (which house Orchid and Hibiscus Gardens), and the National Mosque of Malaysia. Alternatively, the park offers shuttle tram services every day between 09:00 and 18:00, with tickets priced at RM6 for adults and RM2 for children.

ASEAN Sculpture Garden at Tun Abdul Razak Heritage Park is accessible via the LRT rail service. Alight at either Masjid Jamek or Pasar Seni LRT Stations and the park is about 15 minutes away on foot. If you're travelling via the popular KL Hop-On-Hop-Off Tour bus, disembark at Stop 14, which puts you at the main entrance.

ASEAN Sculpture Garden
Opening Hours: Daily 09:00 18:00
Location: Jalan Cenderasari, Taman Botani Perdana, Kuala Lumpur
Tel: +603 2693 4799

Badan Warisan Malaysia in Kuala Lumpur

Badan Warisan Malaysia is home to the Heritage of Malaysia society. Set in the shadow of the PETRONAS Twin Towers, the main building is called the Heritage Centre. It is a bungalow built in 1925 that hosts regular art exhibitions on historic Malaysian buildings, and their environs.

The group's motto is 'Giving our past a future' and the non-governmental organisation has played an important role in the preservation and conservation of the country's architectural heritage since 1983. Besides the art exhibition in the main gallery, Badan Warisan Malaysia hosts monthly talks and lectures.

Rumah Penghulu Abu Seman

Another interesting feature within the Badan Warisan Malaysia grounds is the meticulously-restored Rumah Penghulu Abu Seman (Headman Abu Seman's Home). Originally built in Kedah between 1910 and 1930, it relocated to here in 1996: it is a handsome example of a restored Malay-style wooden house of a local Malay chief. Also within the property's grounds is the Heritage Garden which has a selection of herbs and plants indigenous to the country.

Daily guided tours of Rumah Penghulu Abu Seman are conducted at 11:00 and 15:00 from Mondays to Saturdays. The gift shop inside the Heritage Centre has a beautiful collection of wooden furniture, antiques and local handicrafts for sale.

No. 8 Heeren Street Heritage Centre

The Heritage of Malaysia society also manages the beautifully restored No. 8 Heeren Street Heritage Centre in Malacca (Jalan Tun Tan Cheng Lock), a replica of a two-storey shop-house constructed in the mid-late 1700s. Check out the permanent exhibit at the Badan Warisan Malaysia complex that details the conservation and restoration process of No. 8 Heeren Street Heritage Centre, Malacca, along with shop-house's early history.

Badan Warisan Malaysia

Kuala Lumpur, Malaysia

Opening Hours: 11:00 16:00 Tuesday Saturday
Address: 2 Jalan Stonor Kuala Lumpur 50450
Tel: +603 2144 9273

Batu Caves in Kuala Lumpur

Batu Caves, one of Kuala Lumpur's most frequented tourist attractions, is a limestone hill comprising three major caves and a number of smaller ones. Located approximately 11 kilometres to the north of Kuala Lumpur, this 100-year-old temple features idols and statues erected inside the main caves and around it. Incorporated with interior limestone formations said to be around 400 million years old, the temple is considered an important religious landmark by Hindus.

Cathedral Cave the largest and most popular cavern in Batu Caves houses several Hindu shrines beneath its 100-metre-high arched ceiling. At the foot of Batu Hill are two other cave temples the Art Gallery Cave and Museum Cave which houses numerous Hindu statues and paintings.

Batu Caves is the focal point of the annual Hindu festival of Thaipusam, which attracts thousands of devotees and visitors. Usually held at the end of January, the procession begins on the evening before the Thaipusam Festival at the Sri Mariamman Temple in KL city centre.

The procession more often than not, arrives at Batu Caves in the wee hours of the morning the next day; the entire celebration commences then and is a colourful event that lasts a total of eight hours. In the past the festival has attracted more than one million pilgrims, making it one of the largest gatherings in the world.

Kavadis

Many disciples carry their offerings containers of milk to the Lord Muruga on large, brightly decorated 'kavadis'. Kavadis are two huge semicircular ornate pieces of wood or steel which are bent and attached to a cross structure that can be balanced on the shoulders. These frameworks are also usually combined with various metal hooks and skewers which are used to pierce the skin, cheeks and tongue. The kavadi is decorated with flowers and peacock feathers and some can weigh up to as much as 100 kilos.

Some disciples also fulfil vows that they have made to the Gods by having their bodies pierced by hooks, needles and even skewers and visitors are often fascinated by the dedication of devotees.

The truly amazing feat is when followers begin the arduous climb up the 272 steps to the top of the caves the trek requires a stunning amount of endurance as they often have to work against the press of the bustling masses. Priests wait at the top to sprinkle consecrated ash over the hooks and skewers piercing the devotees flesh before they are removed.

Batu Caves
Opening Hours: Daily, 06:00 - 21:00
Address: Batu Caves, Sri Subramaniam Temple, Kuala Lumpur, Malaysia
Tel: +603 2287 9422

How to get there: 13km north of Kuala Lumpur How to get there: Take Intrakota bus No 11D from the Central Market or the Cityliner bus No 69 at Jalan Pudu to get to Batu Caves. Taxis are also available anywhere around city.

Thaipusam in Batu Caves

Thaipusam is a colourful annual celebration in honour of the Hindu god Subramanian, with festivities mainly taking place in Batu Caves a limestone hill with a series of caverns and temples about 13km north of KL. It is a famous festival largely because of the practice of devotees who impale their bodies with long metal skewers during the event.

Celebrated by the city's Indian community, Thaipusam is one of the best times to visit Batu Caves. 272 stairs lead to the top and just inside the front door, piles of stone slabs have fashioned out a sort of Norman arch that frames a giant, granite-carved statue of Lord Subramanian. Inside the caves are more exquisitely carved Hindu guardian figures; some statues at Batu Caves, like the four-armed depiction of Prithvi, look deeply peaceful while others (such as the giant, green-skinned Lord Hanuman) are intimidating.

Thaipusam takes place between January and February, with thousands of devotees attending each year. The event is not restricted solely to Hindus you will see plenty of tourists merrily snapping pictures: in fact, the warmth and hospitality you encounter here will make you want to never go back.

The Thaipusam festivities actually take place over three days. They start out in the wee hours of the morning (04:00) with a procession from Sri Mahamariamman Temple Kuala Lumpur's oldest Hindu temple in Chinatown. Carrying a golden chariot with a statue of Lord Subramanian, it is accompanied by several hundred worshippers and arrives at Batu Caves by noon. This is when the revelry really gets started...

The main event takes place at the base of the hill: once the statue arrives, devotees start preparing to perform ritual acts of thanksgiving or penance. First, priests 'bathe' them in the river by the caves, with many of them going into 'trances' from the ritualistic prayers. They are then lanced and skewered with metal hooks or spikes a painless process because of the trance.

Family and friends then guide devotees up the stairs to the main grotto of the caves, where they perform more prayers. Besides impaling themselves, followers also carry giant metal constructions (called kavadis) with offerings such as flowers and milk to the top of the caves. Some kavadis can weigh up to as much as 100 kilos. Once prayers are completed, those with skewers attached to their bodies have them removed and their wounds are treated. The event continues throughout the night and into the next day with many queuing up to carry their kavadis up to the central cavern.

After two days at Batu Caves the procession returns to Sri Mahamariamman Temple with thousands of people walking alongside it and performers keeping morale up with drums beating out a driving rhythm.

Some people like to visit Batu Caves at night during Thaipusam when the crowds are thinner and the air is less humid, but we recommend you stop by during the day, when the atmosphere is more electrifying. This is also the best time for photos, when things are very colourful and busy.

It might rain but the brief bursts will almost certainly do nothing to dampen the spirits of followers as they rush to complete their prayers before the end of the three days. But do take an umbrella, just in case.

Thaipusam in Batu Caves
Highlights: 31st January 2018
Location: Batu Caves
How to get there: There are bus services that can take you all the way up to Batu Caves during Thaipusam: simply look for the bus with the paper signage stuck to

its window that says 'Batu Caves' or 'Thaipusam'. They start out at the stand near the Pasar Seni LRT station (behind Sri MahamariammanTemple) and the tickets cost RM2 per one-way trip.

Berjaya Times Square Theme Park

Berjaya Times Square Theme Park is the largest indoor theme park in Malaysia. Located within Berjaya Times Square Hotel, one of the biggest shopping malls in the country, the expansive amusement park is located on the fifth floor and is designed for both adults and children with two zones.

It's perfect for those bad weather days when you can't explore the city centre, or if you're in the mood for a hair-raising roller coaster ride in the midst of a shopping spree after all, it's bound to be less frightening than all the money you're spending in the mall. Highlights include thrilling rides such as the Supersonic Odyssey and DNA Mixer.

The 380,000sqft park is divided into two sections: the Galaxy Station is made for adults while Fantasy Garden is decidedly kid-centric. All in all, there are a total of 14 rides and in comparison to other theme parks around the world, it's pretty limited but Berjaya Times Square Theme Park's saving grace is its easy accessibility and all-weather rides. There are four thrill rides and each has been exclusively designed for Berjaya Times Square Theme Park's World. Galaxy Station sees the most visitors on a weekly basis, but is off-limits for those below the age of 13.

Signature attractions include the 800m long Supersonic Odyssey roller coaster. This custom-made looping ride is the biggest indoor roller coaster in the world and has three inversions: a heart line roll, loop and corkscrew. Additional rides include the 30m high Spinning Orbit, DNA Mixer, Ooort's Express, Dizzy Izzy, and the swinging Space Attack. Topping it all off is the park's latest attraction, the Haunted Chamber this walk-through attraction has actors and special effects to guarantee a goose bump inducing time.

Meanwhile, the Fantasy Garden has eight rides for very young children perfect for families. The colourful Garden Avenue is especially popular with toddlers and other fun rides available include the Crazy Bus, Buddy Go Round, Flying Bumble Bee, Botanic Drive, Molly-Cool's Swing, Fantasy Trail, Robo Crash, and Honey Bump.

Berjaya Times Square Theme Park also has party rooms for birthdays, a 'Kidz Theatre' plus a host of amenities to keep visitors comfortable. The entry fee is worth it for an afternoon's fun especially the thrill rides.

Berjaya Times Square Theme Park
Opening Hours: Monday - Friday 12:00 22:00,
Saturday & Sunday 11:00 22:00
Address: Level 5, Berjaya Times Square, No.1, Jalan Imbi, Kuala Lumpur
Tel: +603 2117 3118

Blue Coral Aquarium at KL Tower

Blue Coral Aquarium at Menara KL Tower is one of the many attractions you can find at the city's iconic landmark, making it a popular spot when you're sightseeing in Kuala Lumpur city centre. Some of its most unique inhabitants include the spotted cardinalfish, fire clownfish, Percula clownfish, skunk clownfish, baby white tip reef sharks, carpet anemones, sand anemones, and porcupine pufferfish

Blue Coral Aquarium at KL Tower Highlights

This compact aquarium houses a variety exotic sea creatures from Fiji, Hawaii, and the Caribbean Islands, with English descriptions of each species displayed in front of the tanks. A guide is also available to provide additional information for those looking to learn more about these sea creatures.

Open daily, tickets are priced at RM18 for adults and RM15 for children. The best way to make your way here is via monorail alight at the Bukit Nanas or Raja Chulan station and Menara KL Tower is less than two kilometres away. Blue Coral Aquarium at Menara KL Tower is also within a five-minute walk from prominent landmarks such as KL Forest Eco Park, KL Tower Mini Zoo, and Kuala Lumpur Upside Down House.

Blue Mosque Selangor

Blue Mosque Selangor is Malaysia's largest mosque and widely considered to be one of its most beautiful. Drawing its name from its impressive blue and silver dome, the mosque has four minarets merging both Malay and Modernist influences into its distinctive architecture.

Blue Mosque Selangor Highlights

This mosque is located in the Selangor's capital city of Shah Alam. It is Malaysia's largest mosque and the second largest in all of Southeast Asia and, not surprisingly, is the city of Shah Alam's most popular tourist attraction. The mosque's 51.2m diameter is the largest religious dome in the world and the four 142.3m minarets are also the tallest in the world. This mosque has an impressive maximum capacity of 24,000 people!

It is not surprising that such a large mosque is visible from many points of the Kuala Lumpur and itself offers beautiful views of the landscaped Garden of Islamic Arts which it overlooks. The mosque isn't difficult to locate given its imposing stature and central Shah Alam location at the end of Persiaran Masjid approximately 40 minutes' drive from KL city centre.

Blue Mosque Selangor
Opening Hours: Monday to Sunday 9:00-13:00 and 14:00-18.30, Friday 9:00-midday and 15:00-18.30
Location: Persiaran Masjid St., Sekysen 14, 40000 Shah Alam, Selangor, Malaysia
Tel: +60 3-5519 9988

Kuala Lumpur Little India Brickfields

Little India Brickfields is a vastly different world than nearby Bangsar. Brickfields is Malaysia's official Little India and used to be a simple residential neighbourhood just outside KL but was recently transformed into a wide street with Indian stores and restaurants run by the country's Indian community.

The shops here sell everything from traditional Indian goods such as saris, flower garlands, spices and Bollywood music, to local delicacies such as vadai, thosai (Indian pancakes made from fermented rice flour) and more. Since its transformation, Little India Brickfields has turned into one of KL's trademark tourist hotspots not only because of the wares found here but for its proximity to KL Sentral station.

History of Little India Brickfields

The original Little India used to be located along Jalan Tunku Abdul Rahman in central KL. Reminiscent of a Middle Eastern bazaar, its main street was known as Jalan Masjid India. Then, in 2009, Malaysian Prime Minister, Datuk Seri Najib Tun Razak announced that the country's official Little India would be moved to Brickfields one of the oldest Indian settlements in the country.

The RM35 million project was undertaken because this generously proportioned boulevard from Jalan Travers up to Jalan Tun Sambanthan could house more colourful cultural stores than KL's busy city centre.

The New Little India

Brickfields' launch as Malaysia's new Little India was jointly unveiled by Indian Prime Minister Manmohan Singh and Malaysia's PM. The showcase included a fireworks display and performances by prominent local Indian artists including renowned classical dancer Ramli Ibrahim as well as Datuk David Arumugam, Jacklyn Victor and Yogi B.

Little India now spans from Jalan Travers to Jalan Tun Sambathan; there's a 35-foot fountain at the junction, an information kiosk at Jalan Thamby Abdullah and a three-storey Indian bazaar at the end of Jalan Tun Sambanthan. The brick-paved Jalan Tun Sambanthan is lined with white street lamps and creamy-yellow arches with purple embellishments to match the newly painted purple buildings along the street.

Little India teems with men on job contracts from India, Bangladesh and Sri Lanka who work at and run the quarter's restaurants and stores. Vendors blasting Bollywood music with rows of Indian CDs on makeshift tables, flower garlands hanging from racks and colourful stacked saris make for a spectacular photo opportunity. In addition, Brickfields is popular for its affordable eateries: most importantly, restaurants specialising in banana leaf lunches and thosai. Many of the businesses here operate late into the night and some even run round the clock.

Traffic used to slow down to a messy crawl and cars would park haphazardly along the streets of Brickfields, so in order to curb congestion a multi-storey car park has been erected near the Kuala Lumpur City Hall sports complex. Still, it's easier to take the Light Rail Transit to get there simply get off at the Sentral LRT

Station and Little India is a short walk away, just outside the terminal.

Brickfields
Opening Hours: 10:00 21:00
Location: Jalan Travers to Jalan Tun Sambanthan, Brickfields

Buddhist Maha Vihara Temple

Buddhist Maha Vihara Temple is a place of worship that practices the Sri Lankan Theravada Buddhist tradition. Also known as the Brickfields Buddhist Temple, it's accessible within a five-minute walk from KL Sentral station. Another one of its biggest selling points is that it has the advantage of not being crowded (compared to most temples in Kuala Lumpur), unless you're visiting during annual festivities, such as Wesak Day or Chap Goh Mei.

Located far away enough from the main streets to provide it with a peaceful atmosphere, the rusty-red and white shrine may appear small on the outside, but it's actually a walled-in structure of high ceilings, ornate fixtures, and impressive reclining Buddha statues. There's also a bookshop selling various publications on Buddhism and sculptures of Buddha at reasonable rates.

Every 1st and 15th day of the Lunar month, local devotees flock to the Buddhist Maha Vihara Temple between 19:30 and 20:30 to present a variety offerings to the statue of Buddha, including flowers, incense, candles, fruits, and sweets. The service is then followed by a recital of Buddhist verses, sermon and blessing by resident monks in the temple.

If you're looking to learn about the religion, the senior resident monks also provide meditation courses, as well as counsel for personal issues such as marital problems, depression, and anxiety for free, but donations are highly welcomed.

Buddhist Maha Vihara Temple
Opening Hours: Daily 06:00 22:00
Address: 123 Jalan Berhala, Brickfields, Kuala Lumpur

Kuala Lumpur, Malaysia

Tel: +603 2274 1141

KLCC - Bukit Bintang Walkway in KL

The KLCC - Bukit Bintang Walkway is a 1.173km-long pedestrian bridge that connects Pavilion KL to Impiana KLCC Hotel and the Kuala Lumpur Convention Centre. The other portion of this walkway is a pedestrian tunnel on the convention centre's concourse level linked to Suria KLCC shopping centre.

Also known as the Pavilion-KLCC pedestrian bridge, there are several entrance and exit points (escalators and staircases) along the bridge: one is located at Connection (an al-fresco dining and entertainment strip at Pavilion KL), while the others are at busy areas such as Jalan Pinang, Jalan Perak, Jalan Raja Chulan and the KL Convention Centre. Also accessible via this bridge is the Raja Chulan monorail station and the KLCC LRT station.

Tourist Friendly

With the KLCC - Bukit Bintang Walkway, people can travel safely, conveniently and comfortably on foot from Bukit Bintang all the way to the Kuala Lumpur city centre, and vice versa. In short, the bridge links the Kuala Lumpur city centre (KLCC) and Bukit Bintang: two major retail and tourism spots. It takes 15 to 20 minutes to walk across the five-metre wide, air-conditioned bridge.

Meanwhile, from the KL Convention Centre, it takes visitors less than a few minutes to access a number of KL landmarks such as the Suria KLCC shopping centre, PETRONAS Twin Towers, KLCC Park and more.

Opened in January 2012 by Prime Minister of Malaysia, Datuk Seri Najib Tun Razak, the RM100 million bridge was a project funded by Malaysian oil giant, Petronas, as a safe, comfortable and convenient alternative to the city's busy roads for pedestrians.

From the KLCC - Bukit Bintang Walkway, you can see the KL City Walk, a 1,200ft-long F&B, retail and entertainment strip located between the KL Convention Centre and Jalan P. Ramlee. Photo enthusiasts will be glad to know that the bridge offers some pretty good views of the KL city centre's architecture.

Bukit Bintang - KLCC Pedestrian Walkway
Opening Hours: Daily 06:00 23:00
Location: Kuala Lumpur City Centre

Bukit Jalil National Sports Complex Malaysia

The Bukit Jalil National Sports Complex (locally called Majlis Sukan Negara) is Malaysia's largest sports and events venue, housing a number of stadiums, parks, and courts for different sports atop Bukit Jalil Hill in Kuala Lumpur. While it's open to the public daily, operational hours depend on the event that are taking place at the venue's many stadiums and sports centres.

The biggest stadium within this complex is the Bukit Jalil National Stadium, which accommodates up to

100,000 people at a time. Constructed in 1998, a standout feature here is the massive sculpture of a keris (traditional Malay dagger) at the stadium's entrance which symbolises courage and heroism in Malay culture.

Bukit Jalil National Sports Complex Malaysia Highlights

Various recreation activities have taken place in Bukit Jalil National Stadium, including music concerts, football events, Commonwealth Games in 1998, and the biannual Southeast Asian Games in 2001, 2009, and 2017.Bukit Jalil National Sports Complex also houses Axiata Arena (formerly called Putra Indoor Stadium), National Hockey Stadium, National Aquatic Centre, and the National Squash Centre.

There's also a recreational park with manmade ponds and jogging tracks within the premise for those looking to enjoy some family-friendly activities, as well as the Bukit Jalil Golf and Country Club for golf enthusiasts. Located along Jalan Barat, Bukit Jalil National Sports

Complex is reachable from Kuala Lumpur city centre via LRT rail services.

Bukit Jalil National Sports Complex
Opening Hours: Daily
Address: Jalan Barat, Bukit Jalil, Kuala Lumpur
Tel: +603 8994 4660

Bukit Jalil Golf & Country Resort KL

Bukit Jalil Golf & Country Resort offers much more than its titular 18-hole golf course. A broad selection of activities is available, from tennis, badminton and squash, to an Olympic-sized swimming pool, a sauna and a gym, there is something to engage every family member. The resort even has a mini bowling alley on site. Professional coaches are also available for private golf lessons and there are group classes in everything from Taekwondo to belly dancing. The course itself was designed by Australian Max Wexler, and is best described as being tough but not daunting, offering many different challenges even for the most seasoned golfer.

Bukit Jalil Golf & Country Resort Highlight

The resort also boasts a range of dining options with three restaurants offering a choice of Malay, Western and Chinese cuisine. The resort also has accommodation in the form of bungalows to suit individuals, couples or family needs. Bukit Jalil Golf & Country Resort is conveniently located 15 minutes from the city center or a short 30-minute drive from Kuala Lumpur Airport via the Seremban and Kesas Highway.

Bukit Jalil Golf & Country Resort
Opening Hours: Hours: Open Daily 11:30-21:00
Location: Jalan Jalil Perkasa 3,Bukit Jalil, Bukit Jalil Golf & Country Resort, 57000 Kuala Lumpur, Wilayah Persekutuan Kuala Lumpur, Malaysia
Tel: +60 3-8996 1841

Bukit Unggul Country Club

Bukit Unggul Country Club Is an 18-hole Golf Course designed by the renowned US architect Ronald Fream. The club welcomes both visitors and members every day. The club boasts a wide range of amenities, including a golf shop, a fully equipped fitness centre, swimming pool, sauna and snooker room. Golf clubs are also available for hire, as are electric carts for getting around the 71 par, 5858-meter-long course.

Bukit Unggul Country Club Highlight

The course itself is located in the hills that overlook the nearby town of Dengkil providing a scenic and challenging 65-hectare course for the beginner and more experienced golfer. Fees vary across the week with Monday and Tuesday being the least expensive days and prices gradually increasing to weekend peaks.

The Bukit Unggul Country Club is located approximately 1 hour drive from Kuala Lumpur City Centre in the major development hub that is known locally as the Multi-Media Super Corridor and comprises Putrajaya, Cyberjaya, and Kuala Lumpur International Airport.

Bukit Unggul Country Club
Opening Hours: 6.30-21:00 Daily

Location: Lot PT 2180-2182, Mukim Dengkil, Daerah Sepang, 43807 Sepang
Tel: +603 89202888

Cathedral of St. Mary in Kuala Lumpur

The Cathedral of St. Mary is one of the oldest Anglican churches in Malaysia and is a KL landmark. Built in 1894 by the British colonial administration, it is located towards the far north side of Dataran Merdeka and looks every inch the typical, picturesque English country church.

A fine example of early English gothic architecture, it started off as a simple timber building in the 19th-century but quickly transformed into a beautiful whitewashed structure with stained glass windows, tasselled tile paving and buttresses. In the old days, the church welcomed the city's European inhabitants every Sunday, and when the service was over they then went to the Royal Selangor Club, which still stands next door.

The Cathedral of St. Mary still maintains a small congregation for the Anglican Diocese of West Malaysia. The beautiful pipe organ was built in 1895 by Henry Willis, a famous English organ builder of his day, who also made the organ for London's St. Paul's Cathedral as well as the original Grand Organ of the Royal Albert Hall.

Visitors are allowed to visit the church and it is usually open throughout the day. The best way to get to the Cathedral of St. Mary is to hop into a taxi: there are several buses that run routes past Dataran Merdeka but you will still have to walk a short distance to the church.

Cathedral of St. Mary
Location: Jalan Raja
Tel: +603 26945470 or +603 2692 8672

Central Market Kuala Lumpur

Central Market is one of KL's most familiar landmarks and a popular tourist attraction. Built in 1928, it is a short walk away from Petaling Street, along Jalan Hang Kasturi. Also called Pasar Seni, it used to be a simple wet market but in the early 1980s was revamped into a handicrafts outlet.

The focus for the city's artistic community, inside the building is a warren of boutiques, handicraft and souvenir stalls with traders selling local merchandise such as authentic Malaysian batik prints and more. Central Market is located on the opposite bank of the Dayabumi Complex and is an art-deco style building with local 'Baroque' trimmings.

Central Market- A Heritage Site

A Malaysian cultural landmark, Central Market has been classified as a Heritage Site by the National Heritage Department. Similar to London's Covent Garden or San Francisco's Fisherman's Wharf, the 120 year-old Central Market has undergone several renovations over the years to attract younger generations and to foster greater appreciation for racial tolerance and integration.

Central Market is strategically located close to major public transportation links, making it easy to access from all major KL destinations. The second floor has several restaurants and a food court serving Asian cuisine.

Cultural Celebrations

Central Market hosts a variety of vendors that bring out their best wares during the country's colourful and exciting annual festivals such as Hari Raya, Chinese New Year and Deepavali. For example, during the Hari Raya festival vendors will sell an assortment of sweet cakes and titbits; at Deepavali, the market has a colourful collection of saris and other Indian merchandise on display, while Chinese New Year sees the bazaar filled with Chinese treats as well as traditional Chinese costumes for sale. For the rest of the year Central Market supports local contemporary arts by hosting art exhibitions.

Merchandise at Central Market

Another way to describe Central Market is to say that it is like New York's SoHo flea market the merchandise here is cheap and traditional goods such as batik, embroidery carvings, souvenirs, and sculptures are on offer. The Batik Emporium houses well-known batik designer labels, while outside local artists painting renderings of the busy street or impromptu song-and-dance performance take place.

Divided into different zones, vendors' stall zones are distinctive by race: the purpose of this zoning practice is to let visitors get an insight into the cultural differences of the various races in Malaysia. There is even a Malacca 'Jonker Street', an area of Central Market that looks like a typical Baba-Nyonya house with Peranakan-style furnishings and fixtures on sale.

Central Market
Highlights: Arch Collection, Actop Craft, Asli Craft, Borneo Pearls, Cute Fish Spa, Dodo Art & Craft, Fine Batik, House of Silver, Kheng's Antique and Collectible, Success Portrait, Suria Portrait Centre, Swartz Creation.
Opening Hours: Daily, 10:00 22:00

Kuala Lumpur, Malaysia

Location: Just around the corner from Kota Raya Shopping Centre
Address: No. 10, 1st-3rd floor, Jalan Hang Kasturi
Tel: +603 2031 0399 or +603 2031 5399 or +603 2031 7399

Chan See Shu Yuen Temple in Kuala Lumpur

Chan See Shu Yuen Temple is one of the largest and oldest surviving Buddhist temples in Malaysia. Located at the southern end of Jalan Petaling, it is characterized by a typical open courtyard and symmetrical pavilions, and decorated with colourful paintings, woodcarvings and ceramic fixtures.

Built between 1897 and 1906, it is quite an elaborate temple: from outside you can see the intricately carved kwang-tung roof, gables and specially-crafted terracotta friezes with monumental Chinese history and mythological scenes. The interior of the main temple has pillars with scenes of gold-painted warriors battling lions, dragons and other mythical creatures.

Design of Chan See Shu Yuen Temple

Behind a glass wall in the main temple are statues of the Chan See Shu Yuen Temple's three main deities, including Chong Wah, an emperor of the Sung Dynasty; above them is a mural of a brilliant yellow sun.

Meanwhile, decorating the edges of Chan See Shu Yuen Temple are blue ceramic vases and small statues of peasants (guardians of the temple) armed with poles crowned with lanterns; on either side of the entrance gate are shrines to the male and female guardians.

Chan See Shu Yuen Temple serves a dual function as both a shrine and a community centre. Originally built as a kongsi (clan house) for families with the surnames Chan, Chen or Tan, the clan founders are depicted at the central altar of the temple. Besides the temple's beautiful architecture you can also see black-and-white pictures (some are hand drawn) of deceased clan members above the altars on the right and left of the main temple during your visit to the temple.

Chan See Shu Yuen Temple is easily accessible via the Pasar Seni LRT: it is only a 15-minute walk from the station.

Chow Kit Market in Kuala Lumpur

Chow Kit Market is recognised as one of Malaysia's most infamous landmarks. Located at the northern end of Jalan Tunku Abdul Rahman, it is divided into two halves: the first half is home to the city's unofficial Red Light District, while the other part is KL's most popular local market.

Even though it is not as well known to tourists as its starlet cousin, Petaling Street (which is located within the same area), Chow Kit Market is definitely exciting. However it is not a place for the faint hearted, with vendors who are pushy and it takes a thick skin to get serious bargains here.

The spotlight on Chow Kit Market focuses on its main street: a lively and culturally-enriching scene. Although the area may not be the most kosher quarter of KL it plays host to the largest wet market in Malaysia. Also known as the Bazaar Baru Chow Kit, this rustic makeshift market is a kaleidoscope of colours and fragrances.

The bazaar is shaded by oversized, colourful umbrellas and divided into a wet and dry section with the colourful souk commonly frequented by locals, especially the neighbourhood's Malay community.

The dry section is without a doubt the cleaner part of the market and more appropriate for tourists: this section has a maze of stalls with fruit, vegetables, tofu, spices as well as clothes, shoes, CDs, DVDs and textiles. Vendors here are polite and this is one of the areas where you can see Malaysian hospitality at its best. Meanwhile the wet market has stalls that sell a variety of meat, from fish and chicken to beef, mutton and pork. Naturally it smells quite strongly, but locals unfailingly frequent this section of the market for the dirt cheap prices.

Red Light District

The other half of Chow Kit resembles Amsterdam's Red Light District though it is not as prolific or as seedy. The notorious side avenues house a labyrinth of buildings that are home to some of the area's more shady 'businesses' including, but not limited to, 'working girls' who hover near doorways along the inner lanes and try to solicit customers. Though Chow Kit is slightly dodgy, with many Malaysians lamenting this area for its sleazy reputation, its presence enriches the city's tourism scene.

Chow Kit Market
Opening Hours: 09:00 17:00
Location: Jalan Haji Hussein, Chow Kit

Dayabumi Complex Kuala Lumpur

Dayabumi Complex is a 35-storey building set along Jalan Sultan Hishamuddin, south of Merdeka Square. Built in the 1970s, it was the first modern building in KL to incorporate principles of Islamic design into its architecture. A major landmark in KL it was one of the city's earliest skyscrapers.

Also known as Menara Dayabumi, the 515ft skyscraper was built to resemble a mosque. Spread across 1,621,930sqft, the Dayabumi Complex has patterns of eight-pointed stars, high vaulted Islamic arches at the top and bottom of the tower and shiny white fretwork (interlaced carved decorative designs). Designed by Malay architect Nik Mohammed, it used to house the headquarters of the national oil company PETRONAS, until they moved to the world famous PETROAS Twin Towers; now it houses several commercial offices.

Dayabumi Complex Kuala Lumpur
Location: Jalan Sultan Hishamuddin

District 21 Kuala Lumpur

District 21 Kuala Lumpur is an adventure theme park set within IOI City Mall Putrajaya, where visitors of all ages can enjoy a variety of challenging obstacle courses. Spanning over 6,500 square metres, the indoor theme park features a post-apocalyptic setting with plenty of metal beams, steel walls and colourful graffiti, as well as suspended ropes, chains, and platforms.

Visitors will first pass through a two-step decontamination chamber, where they are provided with protective gloves and non-slip socks (as shoes are not permitted for certain rides) while staff brief them on the theme park's rules and safety precautions. Fitted with LED-lit climbing walls, high-speed slides, trampolines, and aerial obstacle courses, District 21 Kuala Lumpur boasts 11 attractions with varying levels of difficulty.

The Roller Glider lets you zip-line along curving loops at a speed of 30km/h while Sky Trail has 23 high-altitude rope challenges to test out your stamina and balance. Another popular attraction at District 21 Kuala Lumpur is the Maze, where you navigate your way through a vertical labyrinth of steel tunnels, cages, platforms, and mind-challenging puzzles, some of which are suspended 10 metres above ground.

District 21 Kuala Lumpur is also fitted with a number of kid-friendly rides, including a merry-go-round (Carousel), scaled down rope obstacle courses (Low Ropes), and pedal go-karts within a 100-metre-long track (GoPedal). Parents can be assured of their children's safety as the theme park is well-equipped with auto belays and padded flooring while safety helmets, knee and elbow pads are provided for more challenging attractions.

Entrance fees are RM58 on weekdays and RM76 on weekends while admission is free for wheelchair-bound visitors and children below 90cm in height. Located in Putrajaya, District 21 Theme Park is accessible within a 35-minute drive from Kuala Lumpur International Airport.

District 21 Kuala Lumpur
Opening Hours: Monday Friday 12:00 - 20:00,
Saturday & Sunday 10:00 20:00

Location: IOI City Mall, Putrajaya, Selangor
Address: +603 8328 8888

Firefly Watching & Kuala Selangor Kampung Tour

The Firefly Watching & Kuala Selangor Kampung Tour takes visitors to a wildlife sanctuary in Kuala Selangor, a traditional fishing village about a two-hour drive from Kuala Lumpur city centre. One of the most popular activities you can enjoy during this excursion is cruising along a mangrove swamp and watching the fireflies, but you also have a chance to spot silvered leaf monkeys as well as resident and migratory birds.

This daytrip begins with a pickup from your hotel in Kuala Lumpur, and you'll be chauffeured in a fully air-conditioned vehicle to the quaint village of Kuala Selangor. Fort Altingsburg, built by the second sultan of Selangor in the 18th century, can be found here.

Kuala Selangor Nature Park

At the foot of the fort is the Kuala Selangor Nature Park, which comprises secondary forests, wetlands, inter-tidal mudflats and mangrove swamps. In the middle of the park stands a large aviary housing endangered milky storks, as well as a manmade wading lake which provides an ideal roosting and feeding site for resident and migratory birds from as far away as Siberia.

After the sun sets, your trip continues with a boat ride along the mangrove swamps to catch sight of thousands of luminescent fireflies. Built along the coast, many villages scattered around Kuala Selangor depend on fishing and farming to sustain their livelihood and this tour will let you observe their lifestyle first-hand as they fish, tap rubber and pluck palm oil fruits.

After a filling dinner of freshly-caught seafood at a local restaurant, the night tour ends with a return trip to Kuala Lumpur. The Firefly Watching & Kuala Selangor Kampung Tour is available daily, with tickets priced at

RM205 for adults and RM105 for children between the ages of 3 and 12.

Firefly Watching & Kuala Selangor Kampung Tour
Opening Hours: Daily 15:30 23:30
Location: Kuala Selangor
Price Range: RM205 for adults, RM105 for children (3-12 years old)

Genting Highlands Park

Genting Highlands is the best known of the three hill stations on the western side of the Banjaran Titiwangsa Range. North of KL, it was opened in 1972 and is only 50km away from the Pahang border. One of Genting's most popular features is the Genting Theme Park an amusement park with four zones.

The sizeable hill station isn't like Cameron Highlands or Fraser's Hill it's embraced a glitzy (and slightly cheesy) atmosphere to attract the crowds, and the strategy has worked. There are five hotels on the mountainside but everyday more people show up than they can accommodate.

Genting Highlands Theme Park

Families especially love Gentings mostly because there's so much to do for everyone. Golf courses, a casino, shopping mall and more, keep most occupied but it's the Genting Theme Park that really gets people in. The park is divided into four indoor and outdoor zones the Outdoor Theme Park, First World Indoor Theme Park, Water Park and Video Games Park. The usual thrill rides and water slides are available, but there's also a variety of signature attractions at Genting Theme Park including the Genting Sky Venture a fierce wind tunnel for a simulated skydive plus the fittingly-named Snow World. Food and drinks are expensive considering they only have stuff like hot dogs, sandwiches, juice, soda and more but a day walking in the chilly air can make you hungry, so you'll actually be craving these in no time.

Outdoor Theme Park

By far the park's most popular zone, the Outdoor Theme Park sees the most visitors. It's best to check the forecast before making plans, as bad weather can shut down a number of rides (especially the thrill rides) but on fair-weather days, it's a popular zone for all ages. Queues can be long but, as with most theme parks, the length of the queue is also an excellent gauge to determine the best rides. Attractions with the longest lines include the adrenaline-pumping Space Shot, Corkscrew, Sungai Rejang Flume Ride and Flying Coaster. However, the range of kid-centric attractions is tame in comparison from the spinning Teacups to the Double Deck Carousel. Queues aren't as long and most are safe for kids of all ages (and parents). What's more, the outdoor park has the required assortment of carnival-like games where visitors can win plush toys and more.

First World Indoor Theme Park

After a while the nippy outdoors weather can get to you so it's a good thing that Genting Theme Park has an indoor zone. The First World Indoor Theme Park may not have as many heart-stopping, adrenaline-inducing attractions as its outdoor counterpart but it's still popular no matter the time of day. It's mostly middle-range amusements here bumper cars, gondola rides, carousels, mini trains and more plus there are a lot of shops where you can just browse through looking for clothes or souvenirs. First World Indoor Theme Park's only thrill ride and most popular attraction is the Sky Venture, Asia's first simulated wind tunnel. Besides that, you can put on your winter jackets and snow boots for the snow slide at Snow World.

Water Park & Video Games Park

The chilly air makes most people hesitant about the Water Park, but it's pretty popular with kids after all, which kid isn't enthusiastic about watery fun? There's only one ride here the Rainforest Splash Pool; it's a very large, sheltered heated 'pool' with a water playground, slides and more to keep them occupied. Besides that, the Video Games Park is a loud arcade-style studio with classic games.

Genting Highlands Park

Opening Hours: Outdoor Theme Park:
10:00 18:00 Monday Friday;
09:00 22:00 Saturday, Malaysia School Holiday & Eve of Public Holiday;
09:00 18:00 Sunday & Malaysia Public Holiday

First World Indoor Theme Park:
10:00 24:00 Monday Friday;
09:00 01:00 Saturday, Malaysia School Holiday & Eve of Public Holiday;
09:00 24:00 Sunday & Malaysia Public Holiday

Video Games Park: 09:00 24:00 Monday Friday;
08:00 01:00 Saturday, Malaysia School Holiday & Eve of Public Holiday;
08:00 24:00 Sunday & Malaysia Public Holiday
Address: Genting Highlands, Pahang
Tel: +603 6101 1118

Holy Rosary Church Kuala Lumpur

Holy Rosary Church Kuala Lumpur, built in 1904, is a beautiful Neo-Gothic style monument that caters to the city's Chinese Catholic community. Accessible within a 10-minte walk from Kuala Lumpur KTM train station, it is one of the few best-preserved religious buildings in KL.

Standing out against the countless modern-style condominium, office towers, and hotels nearby the vicinity, the church was blessed by French missionary Father Francis Emile Terrien and is adorned with European-style features such as stained glass windows, a pointed arch, ribbed vault, and flying buttress.

The stained glass windows was designed by Fr. L. Lambert MEP, depicting the five Joyful Mysteries of the Rosary. Set behind the church's main altar, they are also known for its historical value as they had survived the Japanese Occupation of Malaya in 1942.

Set along Jalan Tun Sambanthan, the church is close to several landmarks within Kuala Lumpur City Centre such as National Museum of Malaysia, Planetarium Negara Malaysia, and Sri Kandaswamy Kovil Temple. Do note however, that Holy Rosary Church is only open for mass during weekends and visitors are only allowed photograph its all-white exterior and landscaped garden. If you're planning on visiting the church for mass, the English session is held at 07:00 on weekdays, 17:00 on Saturday, and 08:30 on Sunday.

Holy Rosary Church
Opening Hours: Saturday 17:00 21:00, Sunday 08:30 12:00
Address: 10, Jalan Tun Sambanthan, Kuala Lumpur
Tel: +603 2274 2747

i-City in Shah Alam

i-City Shah Alam is a stunning 72-acre theme park that's well-frequented for its nightly colourful display of LED-lit attractions as well as exciting rides and unique museums. Known as the City of Digital Lights, i City is accessible within an hour's drive from downtown Kuala Lumpur and houses an array of exciting activities, such as a massive water park, 3D and wax museums, and the biggest snow park in Malaysia.

There's also a colourful Ferris wheel, two-tiered carousels and funfair-like booths set up where you can win stuffed toys, while plenty of food stalls and cafes offer an extensive range of local and international delicacies. As the sun sets in I-City Shah Alam, its sprawling 'forest' of artificial maple and pine trees as well as quirky, plastic figures such as peacocks, flamingos, and giraffes are illuminated with millions of LED lights.

Here is the full list of attractions:

- City of Digital Lights
- Red Carpet Wax Museum
- WaterWorld
- SnoWalk
- Trick Art Museum
- House of Horror
- 5D Theatre
- Fun World
- CityWalk
- Space Mission

During the daytime, a visit to WaterWorld is an ideal option as children and adults can play on exciting spiral and rainbow slides and water rides, like River

Adventure through LED-lit caves, a giant Jacuzzi, and the Wave Pool. One of its thrill rides, the Tornado, is a 48-metre water slide with a seven-storey funnel-like tube. Inclined at a 45-degree angle, it starts out 18 metres wide and tapers down to a three-metre wide tube before you splash into a 125 sq. m landing pool.

Hailed as Malaysia's largest snow park, SnoWalk in i-City Shah Alam is a 4,645 sq. m attraction that's decorated with LED-lit igloos, ice houses, slides, a mini-bobsled run, snowmen, ice-carved penguins, and various ice sculptures. Another interesting attraction in this theme park is the Trick Art Museum; a spacious exhibit with unique paintings of wildlife, sculptures and landmarks around the world that seem to come to life when photographed.

The theme park also hosts a Hollywood-themed interactive wax museum, complete with red carpet and a massive golden Oscar statue at the main entrance. Expect life-like wax characters of beloved celebrities and icons such as Michael Jackson, Jackie Chan, Britney

Spears, Steve Jobs, Albert Einstein, and even the royal British family like Prince William and Kate Middleton.

As i-City Shah Alam operates in a cash-free system, guests are required to purchase an i-Card (a prepaid electronic-cash card) to enjoy all the rides and attractions. Not only is it convenient to carry around, you also save loads of time for an adventure-filled day instead of waiting in long queues at the ticket counters.

With a vast array of exciting museums and thrilling rides in a colourful carnival-esque atmosphere, the i-City Shah Alam theme park is perfect for families who want to enjoy an unforgettable experience of fun and adventure in Kuala Lumpur.

i-City Shah Alam
Opening Hours: Monday Thursday 11:00 00:00,
Friday Sunday 11:00 01:00
Address: D-9-1, Jalan Multimedia, 7/AJ City Park, i-City, Shah Alam
Tel: +603 5521 8800

Iron Mosque Putrajaya

The Iron Mosque Putrajaya was built in 2004 with construction finishing in 2009. The mosque is built in a distinctive style that borrows heavily from German and Chinese architectural influences. The most distinguishing features are its lack of a minaret and the fact that it is constructed mostly from steel hence the building's metallic appearance that gives it its name. The mosque was built to hold up to 20,000 worshippers and is also known as Tuanku Mizan Zainal Abidin Mosque.

Iron Mosque Putrajaya Highlights

The mosque is located near the beautiful Poudre Lake and offers panoramic views of the lake and other parts of Putrajaya. Despite being a relatively recent addition to the landscape, its unique appearance has seen it already become a popular tourist destination in the area.

Car parking at the Iron Mosque is located on the lower ground level and you will need to take a lift or escalator to go to the ablution area, which is upstairs. The Prayer Hall is on the next floor up. There is also a children's playground at one end of the mosque.

The Iron Mosque is the Putrajaya's second principal mosque after Putra mosque, even though it covers an area twice the size of Putra's main mosque. It is located opposite the Palace of Justice in Putrajaya's Precinct 3.

Iron Mosque Putrajaya
Opening Hours: Saturday to Thursday 9:00-midday, 14:00-16:00, 17.30-18:00, Friday 15:00-16:00, 17:30-18:00
Location: Jalan Tuanku Abdul Rahman, Presint 3, 62000 Putrajaya, Wilayah Persekutuan Putrajaya, Malaysia
Tel: +60 3-8880 4300

Istana Budaya in Kuala Lumpur

Istana Budaya is Malaysia's National Theatre. Also known as The Palace of Culture, it towers over the National Art Gallery on Jalan Tun Razak. Built in 1999, it is the country's main venue for local and international music, dance and drama performances, including operettas, classical concerts and more.

The first theatre in Asia with state-of-the-art stage equipment, Istana Budaya is rated as one of the world's top 10 most sophisticated theatres, on par with the Royal Albert Hall in London. The RM210 million complex is spread across 54,400sqm and was officially opened by former Prime Minister Tun Dr. Mahatir Mohamad.

Structure of Istana Budaya

Designed by local architect, Muhammad Kamar Ya'akub, Istana Budaya is one of Kuala Lumpur's most striking structures due to its turquoise-blue tiled roof the 'folds' remind one of a giant origami piece. As in a traditional Malay house, the theatre is divided into three areas: the 'serambi' (lobby and foyer), the 'rumah ibu' (auditorium) and the 'rumah dapur' (stage or rehearsal hall).

The main building takes the shape of the 'sireh junjung' traditional betel leaf arrangements used during Malay weddings and welcoming ceremonies with the foyer claiming the spot as the theatre's most intricately designed aspect. Additionally, the main theatre hall (Panggung Sari) which can accommodate up to 1,412 people is a classic opera house with a twist its royal boxes open up like traditional Malay-style windows.

Architecture of Istana Budaya

Istana Negara is vast and opulent, with plenty of white marble and doors made of high-quality tropical wood with hand-carved flowers and leaf designs. The entrance hall has lush carpeting, with the lobby prominently displaying the cempaka flower and beringin tree. The entrance to the theatre is said to be an imitation of a traditional Malay palace noticeably the Balairong Seri at the Istana Negara (National Palace).

Performances at Istana Budaya

Frequent performers at the Istana Negara include the National Theatre Company and the National Symphony Orchestra, whose headquarters are located within the complex. On Saturdays from 11:00 18:00, there is a free live music and dance performance staged in front of the theatre while outside the front gate, cheap food stalls are set up, allowing for one of the city centre's most unique weekly cultural events.

Noteworthy international performances that have taken place at the Istana Negara including The Merchant of Venice by the Royal Shakespeare Company, The Merry Widow, Tosca, La Bohème, Turandot, Carmen and many more. One of its most successful local performances was a production of Puteri Gunung Ledang The Musical, which played to a packed house most nights.

Istana Budaya
Address: 58 Jalan Kuantan Titiwangsa, 53200 Kuala Lumpur
Tel: +603 4026 5555

Istana Negara in Kuala Lumpur

Istana Negara is Malaysia's National Palace. Built in 1928, it is located along Jalan Istana and the 13-acre castle used to be the official residence of the Yang di-Pertuan Agong (King) of Malaysia. In June 2011, it was replaced by a new, extravagant RM800 million palace near Jalan Duta, Kuala Lumpur.

The old Istana Negara is situated on a slope in Bukit Petaling overlooking the Klang River, along Jalan Syed Putra. Its grounds are not open to the public, so the Main Palace Entrance is usually the spot where tourists take pictures. Also called The Big House, it was originally a double-storey mansion owned by local Chinese millionaire Chan Wing.

History of Istana Negara

From 1942 1945, Istana Negara housed the Japanese governor during the Japanese occupation. In 1945, after the Japanese surrendered, the British Military Administration (BMA) commandeered the mansion as a senior military officers' mess. The formation of the Federation of Malaya in 1950 saw the house rented out by the Selangor State Government until Malaysia's independence (merdeka) in 1957.

Later on, Istana Negara was renovated and turned into the Sultan of Selangor's home and in 1957 the property was sold to the Federal Government. Officials then officially converted the building to be used as the residence of the newly-created sovereign post of Yang di-Pertuan Agong of Malaya.

Improvements of Istana Negara

Since then, Istana Negara has undergone much renovation and several extensions, with the most widespread upgrading works carried out in 1980. This was when the first Installation Ceremony for His Majesty DYMM Seri Paduka Baginda Yang di-Pertuan Agong was held at the Istana Negara in 1957. Before this, previous Installation Ceremonies were held at the Tunku Abdul Rahman Hall in Jalan Ampang.

Structure of Istana Negara in KL

The Istana Negara grounds are spread out over 28-acres within the compound is a beautiful garden, swimming pool, six-hole golf course, lake, an indoor badminton court and tennis courts. For safety purposes, there is a guard house for members of the Royal Malay Regiment and at the main entrance, similar to Buckingham Palace, are two guard posts on each side of the arch with members of the cavalry in full dress uniform.

Istana Negara is bordered by a wall with the Malaysian coat of arms, featuring the Royal Insignia of His Majesty, placed on the steel bars between each fenced pillar. The cypress and casuarina-lined driveway leads to two entrances the East Wing and West Wing.

Interior of Istana Negara KL

Istana Negara is divided into two sections: the East Wing and West Wing. The East Wing is home to the Balairong Seri the throne room of the Yang di-Pertuan

Agong, which is only used for official and ceremonial functions. This is the room most often seen in pictures and telecasts of the palace; it sometimes serves as a banquet hall.

The second floor has a few thematic rooms including the Dewan Mengadap, where the King receives honoured guests, the Bilik Duta, a room dedicated to the King's meetings with the Prime Minister and the Bilik Permaisuri, where the Queen entertains her guests. The West Wing of the palace is dedicated to the Bilik Mesyuarat Raja-Raja Kings' meeting room where the Conference of Rulers is usually held.

Like the old palace, the RM800 million complex is not open to the public. Visitors are only able to catch a glimpse of the magnificent and ostentatious complex along Jalan Duta from outside its entrance gates. Works for the construction of the new castle began in mid-2007, with the palace fully completed in June 2011. The old Istana Negara is due to be turned into a museum but peaceful local protest may derail this plan.

Istana Negara
Location: Jalan Istana, Kuala Lumpur

Kidzania Kuala Lumpur

Kidzania Kuala Lumpur (or Kidzania KL) is a memorable, edutainment centre designed to show and encourage kids to 'work' in professional jobs. Teaching them about different career choices, it looks like an indoor city with miniature-sized replicas of office buildings and cars: once you breeze through the AirAsia airport-style entrance, children can take turns performing over 90 different types of grown-up jobs including pretending to be a surgeon, judge, mechanic and hairdresser.

An indoor theme park that first started out in Mexico, today there are several Kidzania Kuala Lumpur experiences around the world and this is Malaysia's first outlet: it is located in Petaling Jaya, about 25 minutes from the KL city centre.

Kuala Lumpur, Malaysia

There are more than 40 'stops' you can make with your offspring it all depends on which jobs catch their fancy. We stopped at the first 'office' the News Straits Times Press building: here, kiddies are given the task of roaming Kidzania to find news to write about and publish, deliver copies of the paper or collect them for recycling from around the city. It is a pretty fun experience for children as they get to sit down for a news brain-storming session and attend a boardroom meeting.

Next up, we dropped in at the Chika's Locker Fashion Boutique a sure-fire hit with little girls: they get to play dress up, learn how to catwalk and model for a fashion parade.

We also loved the office, where kids undergo physical 'tests' to become a certified Kidzania Secret Agent, or have your kid don a pilot's uniform at the AirAsia flight simulator and 'fly' a plane. But by far the most thrilling job is when they get to become honorary fire fighters, ride a fire truck and extinguish a hotel fire. A not-to-bemissed moment comes when kids pretending to be policemen engage in crowd control!

Other highlights include an Actor's Academy, Magic Studio, Surgery Room, C.S.I. Lab, Dentist's Office and Courthouse. Each job a child performs at the two-storey complex earns them Kidzania currency called KidZos. At the end of the day they can redeem merchandise like colour pencils and stationery from the centre's gift store, or even at miniaturized, fast food or sushi places inside Kidzania. It's a great way to teach children the value of money.

Only adults with a kid are allowed entrance into the 80,000sqft Kidzania, and only children can enter 'office' buildings you can watch your child through office windows. An exception to this rule is the Broadcasting Zone, where you get to watch them 'deliver' today's headlines, man the prompter and more.

The best part is that you shouldn't worry about your child's safety as on-site Zupervisors are thoroughly professional and handle kids extremely well. Plus to help you keep track of your child at this busy and popular one-stop learning centre, they have to wear an electronic tracking bracelet that prevents them from leaving Kidzania without their parents.

Kidzania Kuala Lumpur
Opening Hours: 09:00 21:00 Sunday Wednesday;
09:00 23:00 Thursday; 10:00 23:00 Friday & Saturday
Address: Curve NX, 18 Jalan PJU 7/5, Mutiara
Damansara, 47810 Petaling Jaya
Tel: +1300 88 KIDZ (5439)
Price Range: RM55 Kids; RM35 Adults (there is also a drop-off service)

KLCC Park in Kuala Lumpur

KLCC Park is a 50-acre garden set close to Suria KLCC shopping centre. Designed by Roberto Burle Marx, it was designed to provide a touch of greenery for the Petronas Twin Towers and the areas surrounding it. On the park grounds is a 10,000sqm manmade lake (Lake Symphony) with a 43m bridge that cuts across.

Unquestionably, Lake Symphony is the reason most people frequent the park; it has water fountains that can shoot water up to a height of 42m. These daily water shows occur at noon and in the evenings and are popular with kids. KLCC Park has over 1,900 indigenous trees from 74 species; 40 of these trees were transplanted from the former Selangor Turf Club racecourse, which lies to the southeast of the city.

Besides the various waterfalls, fountains, cascade and reflecting pools scattered around the park, there are a variety of facilities at KLCC Park including a two-acre children's playground, a 1.3km-long jogging track, shelters and benches, patterned footpaths and sculptures. On KLCC Park's western stretch is a public children's swimming pool.

KLCC Park
Location: Kuala Lumpur City Centre
Tel: +603 2380 9032

Kuala Lumpur, Malaysia

KL Forest Eco Park (formerly Bukit Nanas Forest

The KL Forest Eco Park, formerly known as the Bukit Nanas Forest Reserve, is one of the oldest permanent forest reserves in Malaysia. Conveniently located beside the Menara KL Tower, this forest reserve covers an area of approximately 11, 0000 sq metres and was founded in 1906, making it the only remaining tropical rainforest in the middle of Kuala Lumpur city centre.

Visitors can find a variety of trees, herbs, bamboo, and creepers, as well as well-maintained walking trails ranging between 300 and 500 metres in length. All trails in KL Forest Eco Park are fairly suitable for beginners and children, plus there are also several facilities within the area, including a playground, campsite, and a wooden gazebo overlooking the Menara KL Tower.

A must-visit here is the Canopy Walk, which is a wood-and-steel aerial bridge that's about 200 metres in height. The bridge towers above the forest reserve, offering sweeping views of Menara KL Tower, and the KL city skyline. The KL Forest Eco Park is open daily and free to enter. It's popular to visit the park in combination with a trip up the Menara KL Tower. A free guided walk is included if you've bought tickets to the tower's observation deck.

KL Forest Eco Park
Opening Hours: Daily 07:00 18:00
Address: Bukit Nanas, Jalan Puncak, Off Jalan P. Ramlee, Kuala Lumpur
Tel: +603 2070 6342

Kuala Lumpur Butterfly Park in Lake Gardens

Kuala Lumpur Butterfly Park is one of the largest butterfly parks in the world, where you can find more than 6,000 live butterflies from 120 species. Located in Tun Abdul Razak Heritage Park (Lake Gardens), it's a popular spot for families and animal lovers looking to escape the bustling KL city centre.

The butterfly park covers over 7,000 square metres and is landscaped like a bushy garden with lots of flowers, vines and exotic plants. The colourful residents are also relatively friendly, some of them even floating to your shirt and hand, sticking like badges. Open daily, the park has with several ponds with cascading waterfalls and unique fountains, which house colourful Japanese koi fish and freshwater turtles.

Kuala Lumpur Butterfly Park Highlights

Besides the butterflies, the park is home to a wide range of preserved insects like rhinoceros beetles and praying mantises, all on display at the onsite museum. There's also a souvenir shop where you can purchased frames of preserved butterflies, scorpions and other insects.

Located along Jalan Cenderasari, tickets to the Kuala Lumpur Butterfly Park are priced at RM25 for adults and RM14 for children aged 3-12. There's an additional fee of RM5 if you bring a video camera to the park, but please note that tripods are not allowed.

Kuala Lumpur Butterfly Park
Opening Hours: Daily 09:00 18:00
Address: Jalan Cenderasari, Taman Tasik Perdana (Lake Gardens)
Tel: +603 2693 4799
Price Range: RM22 for adults, RM11 for children (2 11 years)

Kuala Lumpur City Gallery

The Kuala Lumpur City Gallery is an interesting tourist information centre with a collection of paintings and photos of KL's history, plus miniature mock ups of famous city landmarks. Set in a 114-year old, colonial-style building just beside Dataran Merdeka, this free museum is great if you want to find out a little bit more about KL's history.

The wall with a timeline chronicling KL's history is especially attention-grabbing: it chronicles KL's origins in the 1850s, to the present: the photos of the official groundbreaking of the Petronas Twin Towers are especially interesting. If you are a local, you can't help but feel pride; as a foreigner, you are bound to be awed by Malaysia's milestones.

Some of the photos and paintings (like Malaysia's Independence Day declaration), come with short but informatively written summaries describing the event: others have audio snippets. There is also a 40ft x 60ft scaled model of greater KL and even video footage of important events (like the 16th Commonwealth Games). The museum also has displays on the country's multicultural population, with national costumes like baju kurungs, sarees and cheong sams exhibited.

Be sure to check out the gift store before you leave the locally-made handicrafts like batik, pewter, hand-woven rugs and more, make for good (and cheap) souvenirs. Plus don't miss out on getting a free KL map from the gallery it has interesting city landmarks highlighted for your convenience.

The Kuala Lumpur City Gallery is easily accessible by bus, taxi or LRT. If you take the train, it is an approximate 10-minute walk from the Masjid Jamek station, but if you are using a taxi, just get off at Dataran Merdeka the gallery is just across the street.

Alternatively, the gallery is also on the route of the KL Hop-On, Hop-Off City Tour bus: the nearest stop is a 10-minute walk away.

Kuala Lumpur City Gallery
Opening Hours: 08:00 18:00
Address: 27, Jalan Raja, Dataran Merdeka, Kuala Lumpur
Tel: +603 2698 3333

Kuala Lumpur Convention Centre

Kuala Lumpur Convention Centre, located in the middle of the KL city centre, is a state-of-the-art event space that hosts a variety of activities, conferences, exhibitions, seminars, meetings and entertainment events all year long. Designed and built to world-class standards, it's the first convention centre in Asia to be

'Benchmarked' by Green Globe International (2007) and has won numerous awards since then.

The massive and impressive Plenary Theatre is located on the third floor, and is often used for opening ceremonies, concerts and graduations. There are six exhibitions halls on the ground level that host just about any event, from sports matches to education fairs.

Kuala Lumpur Convention Centre Highlights

Some of the most prominent events that have taken place here include the 11th ASEAN Summit (2005), Global Entrepreneurship Summit (2013) and the 29th Southeast Asian Games' judo, karate and wushu tournaments (2017). Additional facilities within Kuala Lumpur Convention Centre include two ballrooms, a banquet hall, meeting rooms, conference halls, prayer rooms, ATM machines and cafés serving light snacks and coffee.

Visitors are also within walking distances of numerous attractions in the area as Kuala Lumpur Convention Centre is connected to the Suria KLCC Shopping Mall and Aquaria KLCC. It's also right next to the iconic Petronas Twin Towers and KLCC Park, where you can find numerous walking paths, water fountains and trees providing ample shade.

Kuala Lumpur Convention Centre
Opening Hours: Daily
Location: Jalan Pinang, KLCC, Kuala Lumpur
Tel: +603 2333 2888

Kuala Lumpur Upside Down House at KL Tower

Kuala Lumpur Upside Down House at KL Tower is the tallest of its kind in the Malaysian capital, featuring a traditional two-storey English cottage, complete with furniture and home décor that are, as the name implies, completely upside down. Located outside the iconic tower, it's also within walking distances of family-friendly attractions along Jalan P. Ramlee.

The main entrance offers unique photo opportunities, as there's a bright yellow (and upside down) antique car looming above its visitors. Kuala Lumpur Upside Down House is also surrounded by an upside down garden, housing colourful artificial flowers, grass and trees, as well as gazebos overlooking KL City Centre.

Kuala Lumpur Upside Down House at KL Tower Highlights

Inside, visitors can explore a number of rooms that they'd find in a real house, including kitchen, living room, master bedroom and an attic all upside down, of course. One of its most popular photo spots is the baby room, where a variety of toys, clothing and diapers are scattered across the upside down ceiling. Depending on how long you need to pose for photos, a visit here takes between 30 minutes to an hour.

Ideal for travelling families, Kuala Lumpur Upside Down House cost RM20 for adults and RM15 for children. If you're travelling via public transport, the quickest way to get to Menara KL Tower is by monorail, as it is just 2 km away from the Bukit Nanas and Raja Chulan stations.

Upside Down House
Opening Hours: Daily 09:00 19:00
Location: KL Tower, Jalan P. Ramlee, Kuala Lumpur
Tel: +6010 802 7547
Price Range: RM20 for adults & RM15 for children

Kuan Ti Temple in Kuala Lumpur

Kuan Ti Temple is a 121 year-old Taoist temple located along Jalan Tun HS Lee. An easily recognisable building with a bright orange façade, it is dedicated to Guandi, the Taoist God of War and Literature; there is a red-faced, long beard statue of Guandi at the rear of the temple.

Also known as Guan Di Temple, on the altar in front of the statue of Guandi (also called Guan Gong or Guan Yu) is guan dao and guan jie a famous sword and spear. Deified in the Sui Dynasty (580-618 AD), devotees believe that Guandi's weapons have special powers and that they will be blessed by 'touching' or 'lifting' the 59kg copper guan dao three times.

Design of Kuan Ti Temple

Also known as the Kwong Siew Free School, two stone Chinese lions (used as protective symbols to ward off negative energy) on pedestals guard the entrance of the temple. They form a happy, protective 'family' that guards the temple: the male (with a ball) is on the left side of the door, inside looking out, and the female is on the right with a baby Chinese lion.

Behind the two lions are the Door Gods (Men Shen) and two smaller Chinese lions; even the roof is a sight to see with beautiful carvings of dragons and chi lins.

Interior of Kuan Ti Temple

Inside the temple is a counter where joss sticks and incense are sold. Colourful dragons are coiled around the two main pillars in the interior of the temple. By the side of the main Guandi statue at the altar are his two attendants: Guanping (who carries a seal) and

Zhoucang (his standard bearer); the three statues are wooden but as a sign of his elevated status, Guan Di's face is painted gold.

Interesting fact: in China, Guan Di, the patron saint of the martial arts, is extremely popular with the police and triads and both pray to him for divine protection.

Kuan Ti Temple
Opening Hours: Daily, 07:00 19:00 (opening hours may vary, so please check with the temple keeper)
Location: Right across the street from Popular Bookstore, and just opposite Sri Mahamariamman Temple.
Address: Along Jalan Tun H. S. Lee

Kuan Yin Temple in Kuala Lumpur

Kuan Yin Temple was built in 1880 and is dedicated to the Goddess of Mercy, Kuan Yin. Also known as Guanyin Temple, it is located across the road from Jalan Stadium in Chinatown. Featuring distinctly Chinese and European baroque architecture, the temple is one of the most colourful shrines in the city.

Kuala Lumpur, Malaysia

Kuan Yin Temple faces the Bulatan Merdeka roundabout, across the street from the Kuala Lumpur and Selangor Chinese Assembly Hall. Since it is nearby the Masjid Jamek LRT station, it is easy for tourists to get to. Though the temple is not as extravagant as others in the city, it is worth a visit to see the three golden Chinese Buddhist statues inside.

The figure in the main prayer hall is that of Shakyamuni (Gautama Buddha); to his right is the statue of the South Sea Guanyin a robed statue with a flashing halo. To the left of Shakyamuni is Qianshou (Thousand Arm Goddess of Mercy) Guanyin: this statue represents Kuan Yin's compassionate side as the goddess purportedly has a 'thousand hands and a thousand eyes' to generously provide for devotees. At prayer times (12:30 13:45), the chanting of 'Namo Guanshiyin Bodhisattva' from devotees and priests is a beautiful, melodious sound.

Kuan Yin Temple
Opening Hours: 07:00 17:00

Address: Jalan Stadium and Jalan Maharajalela, Chinatown, Kuala Lumpur

Tun Abduk Razak Heritage Park

Tun Abdul Razak Heritage Park offers hours of fun activities and sightseeing opportunities for just about any visitor, from nature lovers to families with little ones. More commonly known as Lake Gardens, this sprawling 227-acre park is located right in the middle of Kuala Lumpur and is reachable via buses, taxis and KTM rail services. The park is open every day between 07:00 and 20:00 and, while it's free to enter, you are required to pay an entrance fee when visiting certain landmarks within the grounds.

One of the largest urban parks in the city centre, it was originally established by the 19th century British state treasurer to Malaya, Alfred Venning, in the 1890s. Among the most significant landmarks in the park, the majestic Carcosa Seri Negara the official residence of former British government representative Frank

Swettenham is located on one of the park's hills. Over the last 20 years, the park's spectacular landscaping has become more impressive.

What to See and Do at Tun Abduk Razak Heritage Park

Today, visitors can find a number of gardens and wildlife sanctuaries that are within walking distances of each other, including the <u>Kuala Lumpur Butterfly Park, Perdana Botanical Garden</u> (which houses the Hibiscus Garden and Orchid Garden), <u>Kuala Lumpur Bird Park and ASEAN Sculpture Garden</u>. Perdana Botanical Garden in Tun Abdul Razak Heritage Park is a favourite picnic spot, with large sculpted vegetation, picnic areas, children's playgrounds and a number of stalls selling food and drink. Most visitors come on the weekends but, due to its sheer size, it doesn't get too crowded.

The main road through Lake Gardens leads to the Tun Abdul Razak Memorial, at the southeast edge of the park. The house is the former residence of the country's second Prime Minister, the late Tun Abdul Razak. He is best known as the 'father of Malaya' and, in recognition of his services, his old house was transformed into a museum of sorts. Inside are preserved documents, speeches, books, awards and his collection of walking sticks and pipes. On the lawn are his well-maintained motorboat and golf trolley. If you're looking to learn more about Malaysia's rich history, you can easily make your way to <u>National Monument, Museum of Islamic Arts</u>, and <u>Parliament House</u>, which are also within the park grounds.

How to Get to and Around Tun Abdul Razak Heritage Park

There are several buses head to the main entrance of Tun Abdul Razak Heritage Park: from Jalan Sultan Mohammed, there is the blue bus #30; from Lebuh Pasar Besar, the pink bus #22 or # 38; from Kotaraya Plaza, bus #21C or #48C; lastly, bus #18 or #21A from Chow Kit. Alternately, the KL Hop-On-Hop-Off stops at the National Monument.

The park is relatively flat with plenty of walking paths and trees providing ample shade, but you can also enjoy daily shuttle tram services between 09:00 and 18:00, with tickets priced at RM6 for adults and RM2 for children.

Tun Abduk Razak Heritage Park
Opening Hours: Daily 07:00 20:00
Address: Jalan Parlimen, Kuala Lumpur
Tel: +603 2691 6011

Lake Gardens Kuala Lumpur Segway Tour

The Lake Gardens Segway tour by Eco Ride Malaysia is a fun and environmentally friendly way to see Tun Abdul Razak Heritage Park's many animal parks, landmarks, and scenic spots. The two-hour tour covers a 10-kilometre sightseeing route within the expansive park, starting at the National Museum (Muzium Negara).

Available by appointment, Eco Ride Malaysia can easily arrange for a pickup from your hotel in KL.

Alternatively, you can meet up with your guide at a specific location in the park. Do note that Tun Abdul Razak Heritage Park is fully outdoors, so we highly recommend choosing either morning or evening sessions to enjoy a more comfortable experience.

Lake Gardens Segway Tour Highlights

There are plenty of photo opportunities throughout your Lake Gardens Segway tour, especially at the Perdana Botanical Gardens, Kuala Lumpur Butterfly Park, and Kuala Lumpur Bird Park. If you're nervous about navigating a Segway, there'll be a helpful guide on hand to lead you through the entire excursion. While you're not travelling at high speed, helmets are provided for added safety.

The tour is priced at RM168 per person, which is inclusive of an English-speaking guide and your Segway vehicle. You are required to pay for your own meals, beverages, and entrance fees to certain attractions within Tun Abdul Razak Heritage Park.

Lake Gardens Kuala Lumpur Segway
Opening Hours: Daily 09:30, 13:00 & 16:30
Location: Tun Abdul Razak Heritage Park, Kuala Lumpur
Tel: +6017 882 3847
Price Range: RM168 per person

Madras Lane Petaling Street

Madras Lane Petaling Street is a narrow alleyway that's known for its tasty hawker fare, as well as a wet market that sells a variety of produce, meat, poultry and fish. Set within Chinatown Kuala Lumpur, it's connected to the Petaling Street Flea Market via a Chinese-style archway bearing the name Penjaja Gallery. Locals frequently refer to the hawker street as Madras Lane after a cinema of the same name, which was destroyed in a fire during the late 1970s.

The wet market gets very busy with locals shopping for groceries, vegetables and meat live chicken and fish are freshly slaughtered here, so it can be upsetting for those with a weak stomach. When you reached the end of the lane, you'll find the food court, which is fitted with food stalls as well as a limited number of plastic tables and chairs.

What to Eat in Madras Lane Petaling Street

The food at Madras Lane Petaling Street is predominantly Chinese, with curry *laksa* and *yong tau foo* being the most popular options among local diners. The former is a mix of noodles, long beans, eggplants, cockles, deep-fried tofu and pork rind, served in a spicy broth that's made with coconut milk and curry.

There are several stalls selling *assam laksa* (Nyonya noodles in spicy and tangy fish soup), so we suggest picking the one that's busiest if you're not pressed for time. A standard-sized dish plus drink at Madras Lane Petaling Street should cost no more than RM10. As Madras Lane Petaling Street is one of the most popular (and inexpensive) breakfast spots in Chinatown Kuala Lumpur, be sure to get there early to avoid a long wait.

Madras Lane Petaling Street
Opening Hours: Tuesday Sunday 08:30 15:00

Location: Lorong Bandar, 20, off Jalan Petaling, Kuala Lumpur

Masjid Jamek Mosque

Masjid Jamek Mosque, also known as Friday Mosque, is recognised as the oldest Islamic place of worship in Kuala Lumpur. Overlooking the Klang River, it offers breathtaking photo opportunities for travellers due to the combination of ancient Moorish, Islam and Mughal architectural styles, verdant surroundings, and distant views of KL's other iconic landmarks.

Built in 1907 by British architect Arthur Benison Hubback, Masjid Jamek Mosque served as the main centre of worship for the local Muslim community until the Masjid Negara (National Mosque) was officially opened to the public in 1965. Surrounding the main prayer hall are three domes, the tallest of which measures at 20 metres, flanked by two brick minarets that stand over 25 metres tall.

A must-visit for those looking to know more about Islam, there's also an Islamic Experience Centre just outside the mosque, which houses a number of informative displays in English. Meanwhile, notable attractions such as Central Market, Chinatown KL, and Petaling Street are easily accessible on foot from the mosque.

Located along Jalan Tun Perak, the best way to get to Masjid Jamek Mosque is via KTM train. Alight at the Masjid Jamek stop and the mosque is right outside the station. While Masjid Jamek Mosque is open to the public daily (apart from Fridays), visitors can only enter the mosque after prayer times.

Robes and headscarves can be borrowed at the mosque's entrance, but we highly encourage visitors to dress conservatively (sleeveless shirts, shorts or skimpy clothing are prohibited) and wear shoes you can easily remove before entering the prayer halls.

Masjid Jamek Mosque

Opening Hours: Saturday Thursday 08:30 12:30 & 14:30 16:30
Address: Off Jalan Tun Perak, Kuala Lumpur City Centre

Masjid Negara Mosque in Kuala Lumpur

Masjid Negara, Malaysia's National Mosque, is the nationwide symbol of Islam. Comprising a main prayer hall with 48 smaller domes around it, it is set to the northwest of the old railway station, a couple of hundred metres towards the end of Jalan Sultan Hishamuddin.

Spread across 13 acres, the National Mosque is able to accommodate up to 15,000 people and is reminiscent of the Grand Mosque in Mecca, featuring abstract shapes and geometric lattice incorporated into its roofing and ironworks. The Grand Hall is undoubtedly the most intricate part of the mosque with verses from the Koran decorating the walls.

The National Mosque

Built in 1965 (the year that Malaysia and Singapore split) it was designed by UK architect Howard Ashley, and Malaysians Hisham Albakri and Baharuddin Kassim. The contemporary-styled Masjid Negara's main dome is star-shaped with 18 points: the points represent Malaysia's 13 states and the five pillars of Islam. It can accommodate up to 8,000 worshippers.

The 73m-high minaret is easily the mosque's most distinguishable feature and a prominent feature of the KL skyline. Also impressive are the beautiful outdoor gardens with white marble pools and fountains. The pink-tiled roof was replaced with blue and green tiles when the mosque underwent extensive renovations in 1987.

There is a seven-point, umbrella-shaped annexe, Makam Pahlawan (Heroes' Mausoleum), towards the back of the mosque that contains the crypt of Tun Abdul Razak, Malaysia's second prime minister, as well as other political celebrities. Fun fact: there is an underground passage that connects the National Mosque to the old railway station.

You can only enter the mosque when prayers are over and visitors must be appropriately dressed. This means that sleeveless shirts, shorts or skimpy clothing are frowned upon; however if you have come ill-prepared, robes and headscarves can be borrowed from the desk at the mosque's entrance gate.

Masjid Negara, Malaysia's National Mosque

Opening Hours: 09:00 23:00 Saturday Thursday;
02:45 18:00 Friday
Address: Jalan Sultan Hishamuddin
Tel: +603 2693 7784

Masjid Raja Fisabilillah Cyberjaya

Masjid Raja Fisabilillah Cyberjaya is the principal mosque of Cyberjaya, a town located 30 km north of Kuala Lumpur International Airport. Also called the Green Mosque, it was constructed in 2006 and named after the former Crown Prince of the Johor-Riau, Raja Haji Fisabilillah ibni Daeng Chelak.

Masjid Raja Fisabilillah Cyberjaya Highlights

It well-regarded as the first mosque in Malaysia to be awarded with a Platinum Green Building Index, using energy-efficient LED lights, natural air ventilation, rooftop solar panels, and rainwater harvesting system to cater to over 5,000 worshippers. Facilities include elevators for the elderly and disabled, a function room for weddings, and a playground for children.

This futuristic mosque hosts a wide range of activities, including Ramadan bazaars, marriage ceremonies, and Friday markets. Masjid Raja Fisabilillah Cyberjaya is also within driving distances of other prominent mosques such as the Iron Mosque and Putra Mosque in Putrajaya. As it's a holy place, do dress conservatively and be courteous to worshippers when visiting the mosque.

Masjid Raja Fisabilillah Cyberjaya
Location: Persiaran Semarak Api, Cyberjaya, Cyberjaya, Selangor
Tel: +60 3 8322 0096

Kuala Lumpur, Malaysia

Megakidz Funland & Edutainment at Mid Valley

Learning doesn't just stop at school, and it can be fun, too! Megakidz Funland & Edutainment offers just that and plenty more for kids and parents alike. Situated on the third level of Midvalley Megamall, this 27,000sqft learning and play centre contains multitude of facilities catering for kids from the age of one to 16. If you're looking for a fun day out with your children without it costing the earth, this might be it.

Every corner of this colourful edutainment centre is filled with funit comprises an aviation play system, a toddlers' corner, an air bouncer, a small cinema and a cafeteria so there's plenty to see and jump around on! The state-of-the-art aviation play system is the biggest in Asia, with its tall slides and pop-up play helicopter, and the toddlers' corner houses a small-scale play system that is designed to help with development and growth. The cinema, on the other hand, has a capacity of up to 50 children, perfect for small movie screenings.

As parental supervision is needed for every child in the Megakidz premises, two adults get in for free per entrance so you will always be able to keep an eye on your children whilst they are playing in the centre. For parents who would like to shop without fuss, there is the 'Drop & Shop' program you can easily drop your kids to for a bit of fun under the supervision of professional guardians for a small hourly rate, and come back again when you're ready. Alternatively, you can also enquire about their half-day and full-day packages if you're planning to spend your day at the mall.

Megakidz emphasize learning by organizing classes tailored especially for kids. Lessons such as dancing, music and Mandarin are mostly conducted during the weekends, in slots of 30 minutes to two hours. Party packages are also available at the centre, and there are rooms made exclusively for this purpose. The packages are according to the number of attendees, and are complete with invitation cards, unlimited playtime at their funland after the party, and party hats and masks.

Pass offers are available all throughout the year, but if you're planning to come back for more, consider taking out membership for your children benefits include free sessions of Drop & Shop, birthday gift vouchers and family member discounts. You can also purchase their weekday and weekend passes for RM100 if a membership sounds too much for you this includes unlimited playtime on multiple days of the week.

Midvalley Megamall is one of the biggest malls in Kuala Lumpur, with 430 shops and F&B outlets under one roof. To get to the mall, you can take the Komuter line and stop at mall's station, Midvalley. There is also a free shuttle bus service available at the nearest LRT station, LRT Bangsar, starting as early at 8:05AM and leaving at 30-minute intervals.

Megakidz Funland & Edutainment
Opening Hours: Monday Sunday 10:00 21:30

Address: Lot T-012, North Court, 3rd Floor, Mid Valley Megamall, Midvalley City, Lingkaran Syed Putra, Kuala Lumpur
Tel: +603 2282 9300

Merdeka Square in Kuala Lumpur

Merdeka Square is undoubtedly KL's best known landmark. Also called Dataran Merdeka, it is set in front of the Sultan Abdul Samad Building (the former State Secretariat). Directly in front is the Royal Selangor Club and to the north is St. Mary's Church, one of Malaysia's oldest Anglican churches.

Within the colonial core of Kuala Lumpur, where the remnants of the British empire are especially evident, Merdeka Square seems to be nothing more than a giant field with perfectly manicured green lawns and a centrepiece of the tallest flagpole in the world (95m) proudly displaying the Jalur Gemilang (Malaysian flag). At the corner of Jalan Tuanku Abdul Rahman and Jalan Raja Laut, Merdeka Square is made up of a padang (field) that was once the Selangor Club cricket pitch.

Colonial Core Surounding Merdeka Square in Kuala Lumpur

Despite numerous changes to its landscape over the years, Kuala Lumpur has retained its majestic charm with Merdeka Square and its colonial surroundings at its heart. The beautifully-tended, 200m-long padang is the most famous stretch of green in KL it was here that Malaysia proclaimed merdeka (freedom or independence) on August 31st, 1957. Beside the lofty flagpole is a giant TV screen with a mix of flashing advertisements and religious messages.

Royal Selangor Club at Merdeka Square in Kuala Lumpur

The venue for Malaysia's annual Merdeka Parade (Independence Day) celebration, Merdeka Square hosts rock concerts and underneath the pitch is the Plaza Putra shopping complex. Meanwhile, directly opposite is the very British Tudor-inspired Royal Selangor Club: built in 1884 it was the favourite watering hole of the British elite and the centre of colonial society in its heyday. The frequent backdrop in most sightseeing photos of Merdeka Square, much of it was destroyed in a fire in the 1960s. The rebuilt club is still a favourite haunt of KL VIPs. The low, black-and-white mock-Tudor building used to be called 'the Spotted Dog' in memory of its mascot a Dalmatian belonging to a former member. Though membership is open to anyone who can afford it, RSC's colonial saloon is still an exclusive haunt and remains an all-male preserve

Menara KL Tower

Along with the Petronas Twin Towers, Menara KL Tower is easily Malaysia's most recognizable and popular landmark. Constructed in 1994, the tower stands at 421 metres and effortlessly trumps the Petronas Twin Towers with the highest and most spectacular view of the city. This gleaming tower's spindle-like apex is visible from almost anywhere in Kuala Lumpur.

Menara KL's viewing deck is, at 276 metres, at least 100 metres higher than the Petronas Twin Towers' Skybridge; the view is marvellous during the day and even better at night when you can see the entire sparkling city centre.

The tower is erected atop the Bukit Nanas (Pineapple Hill) Forest Reserve the oldest gazetted forest reserve in the country, which houses age-old trees as well as flora and fauna indigenous to Malaysia's tropical climate. Primarily used as a communications infrastructure, it is the fifth-tallest telecommunications tower in the world.

When it was originally built, the natural surroundings of Bukit Nanas were kept intact to ensure balance in development; in fact a 100-year-old Jelutong tree was preserved, at great cost, by building a retaining wall around it.

When Menara KL Tower was constructed the overall design was meant to represent the human journey for perfection in life. The tower's architectural-style reflects Malaysia's vibrant Islamic heritage with Arabic scripts, Islamic tiles, and archetypal Islamic floral and abstract patterns.

The structure has 'Muqarnas' a type of corbel used as a decorative device in traditional Islamic and Persian architecture underscoring its design as homage to the revival of Islamic architectural heritage. The main lobby of the upper ground floor is decorated with exquisite glass-clad domes that sparkle like giant diamonds; the tower's familiar globular pinnacle is inspired by a Malaysian spinning top.

Menara KL Tower
Opening Hours: Daily 09:00 - 22:00
Address: Jalan Puncak, Off Jalan P. Ramlee, Kuala Lumpur City Centre
Tel: +603 2020 5444

Movie Animation Park Studios Malaysia

Kuala Lumpur, Malaysia

Movie Animation Park Studios Malaysia is the state's second theme park after Sunway's Lost World of Tambun. A two-hour drive from Kuala Lumpur, it is located in Ipoh, a historical town in Perak that's known for its timeless charm, limestone caves, Buddhist shrines and hot springs.

Spanning over 210,000 square metres, visitors can find about 40 attractions and rides that are divided into six movie-themed zones. The colourful theme park features familiar characters and settings from Hollywood blockbusters, such as The Smurfs, Megamind, Casper and Mr. Peabody & Sherman, as well as local animation BoBoiBoy.

Thrill-seekers can watch high-speed chases and high-risk stunts at the 2,000-seat Stunt Legend Arena, or ride the Megamind Megadrop; a drop tower over 20 floors in height. There are also two indoor rollercoaster rides inspired by The Croods and Casper the Friendly Ghost.

The first of its kind in Asia, Movie Animation Park Studios Malaysia's key attraction is The Smurfs Theatre. It hosts an interactive animated showcase called Papa Smurf's Rainbow Spell, where visitors can explore Papa Smurf's laboratory and help him cast magical spells throughout the show. Meanwhile, younger children can enjoy various rides and slides at The Smurfs Playland.

Movie-themed cafeterias and restaurants are plentiful here, and you can enjoy a variety of local and international fare at reasonable prices. Open daily, tickets to Movie Animation Park Studios Malaysia are priced at RM120 per person and give you unlimited access to all rides for the day. If you're Malaysian, the entrance fees is RM114.

Movie Animation Park Studios Malaysia
Opening Hours: Mon Fri 10:00 18:00, Sat Sun 10:00 22:00
Address: Persiaran Meru Raya 3, Bandar Meru Raya 3, Ipoh, Perak
Tel: +605 501 5630
Price Range: RM120 & RM114 (with valid MyKad)

Kuala Lumpur, Malaysia

Islamic Arts Museum Malaysia

The Islamic Arts Museum Malaysia is one of Kuala Lumpur's most popular attractions, and well-regarded as Southeast Asia's largest museum of Islamic art. Housing extensive collections of Islamic decorative arts from all over the world, this stunning building is located at the fringe of the 227-acre Lake Gardens and is accessible within a five-minute walk from the National Planetarium and National Mosque.

An impressive architectural feat, Islamic Arts Museum Malaysia features a huge blue turquoise dome on top of the building, glass walls that allow natural light to flow in, domed ceilings adorned with intricate Islamic patterns, and a vast exhibition space which spans 30,000 square metres. Housing more than 7,000 artefacts, the permanent galleries are situated on the two upper floors, which span twelve themes:

• Architecture	• Textiles
• Quran & Manuscripts	• Arms and Armour
• India	• Coins and Seals

- China
- Malay World
- Jewellery
- Metalwork
- Ceramics
- Living With Wood

Notable exhibits in Islamic Arts Museum Malaysia include the 1964 Kiswa, which is the exquisite door curtain of the Ka'aba (the House of God) that gets changed annually, and manuscripts such as prayer books dating back to the 17th century. The architecture gallery deserves a mention too; models of impressive mosques all around the world are on display and with high attention to the detail of each building. They include the holiest site in Islam, which is the Sacred Mosque (Al-Masjid Al-Haram) in Mecca, and the Great Mosque of Xian in China.

Islamic Arts Museum Malaysia also hosts additional facilities and activities such as children's library, storytelling sessions every Saturday, as well as arts-and-craft lessons. Visitors craving a bite by the end of their visit at Islamic Arts Museum Malaysia can head to the Museum Restaurant, where they can enjoy dishes from Egypt, Palestine, Jordan, Syria, Lebanon, Turkey and the Arab Gulf.

Located at the Ground Floor, the Museum Shop has a remarkable selection of Islamic crafts and artefacts from around the world, including stationery, tee shirts, books, puzzles, and even intricate jewellery from the Middle East. Overall, The Islamic Arts Museum Malaysia is definitely a pleasant way to spend your afternoon, offering a unique and mesmerising insight into the world of Islam that is not usually seen by the public.

If you're a first-time visitor in Kuala Lumpur, we highly recommend the KL Hop-on Hop-Off Tour, which is a double-decker and air-conditioned tour bus that takes you to over 40 attractions throughout Kuala Lumpur. Best of all, pre-recorded multi lingual commentary is available for each of the attractions, including the Islamic Arts Museum Malaysia.

Caleb Gray

Islamic Arts Museum
Opening Hours: Daily 10:00 18:00
Address: Jalan Lembah Perdana, Kuala Lumpur
Tel: +603 2274 2020

National Monument in Kuala Lumpur

The National Monument is located 50m along Jalan Tamingsabi, at the northern end of the Lake Gardens on Jalan Parlimen. The 15m-high bronze statue is dedicated to the 11,000 people who died during the First World War, the struggle against the Japanese and the Malayan Emergency. Providing excellent views of Parliament House, it was built in 1966 and features the inscription 'To Our Glorious Dead of the First World War (1914-1918), Second World War (1939-1945) and the Emergency (1948-1960).' The world's tallest freestanding bronze sculpture grouping, the monument of seven soldiers standing and supporting their fallen comrades was designed by Felix de Weldon, the same noteworthy designer who worked on the Iwo Jima Memorial in Washington DC. Each figure denotes one of seven qualities: courage, leadership, sacrifice, strength, suffering, unity and vigilance.

History of Malayan National Liberation Army

The Malayan Emergency (also known as the Communist Emergency) was a 12-year battle waged between Commonwealth armed forces and the Malayan National Liberation Army (MNLA), the military arm of the Malayan Communist Party. Unfortunately, though the state of emergency was lifted in 1960, members of the banned Communist Party placed a bomb under the sculpture in 1975 but thankfully the memorial was saved.

The first National Monument, a cenotaph, was set up by the British government to commemorate WWI, WWII and honour the fallen heroes of the Malayan Emergency. The second, and present, RM600, 000 National Monument took over five years to construct.

Sculpture Garden

The National Monument is surrounded by a moat with fountains and ornamental pewter lilies. Just beside the National Monument sculpture is the Asean Sculpture Garden. Here, abstract art pieces made of marble, iron, wood and bamboo, from neighbouring ASEAN (Association of South East Asian Nations) countries are displayed.

The Malaysian Houses of Parliament are situated beside the monument. One of Malaysia's protected landmarks; a soldier raises the Jalur Gemilang (Malaysian flag) at dawn everyday and lowers it at dusk. Every July 31 (Warriors Day), a wreath-laying ceremony takes place at the National Monument. Interestingly, a new monument is set to be built in Putrajaya, the country's administrative capital.

National Monument Kuala Lumpur
Opening Hours: 07:00 18:00
Location: Jalan Tamingsabi
Address: Jalan Parlimen, Kuala Lumpur 50480
Malaysia
Tel: +603-2615-8188

Kuala Lumpur, Malaysia

National Museum in Kuala Lumpur

National Museum is located near the southern tip of the Lake Gardens, past the National Art Gallery. An excellent introduction to Malaysia's history, economy, geography, arts, crafts and culture, it overlooks Jalan Damansara and was built in 1963 with its displays spread out onto three floors.

The building has a sweeping, traditional Minangkabau-style roof and a main entrance flanked by two large murals of Italian glass mosaic that portray the country's major historical events and cultural activities. A couple of years ago the National Museum underwent an extensive renovation that had an all-new gallery added to its complex.

History of National Museum

Much of the National Museum's original collection of artworks was razed during a World War II bombing but the museum still has an extensive ethnographic and archaeological exhibit on display. Its impressive collection starts out on the ground floor with life-sized dioramas of ritual weddings, traditional Malaysian life (fishing, farming, weaving etc.) taking place in kampung settings and even one of a Malay circumcision ceremony.

There is even a life-size, traditional Malacca Baba house with beautiful mahogany furniture, elaborate carpets and brass, silver and gold ornaments on the first floor. Additionally, the museum adds a hint of the prosaic to the mix with a section dedicated to the Malay art of wayang kulit a kind of shadow wooden puppet theatre.

Make Love, Not War

The second floor of the National Museum sees a huge zoological section with stuffed animals it vaguely resembles a hunting lodge. Up here is also a fairly impressive collection of weapons, including parangs (machetes), kris (daggers), swords and miniature canons. Walking down one the winding passages will lead you to a section dedicated to traditional musical instruments including the serunai (a reed with a multicoloured end), rebab (a fiddle played like a cello), rebana (drums), Kelantanese drums and Chinese gongs, lutes and flutes.

The National Museum has several guided tours that take place throughout the week. It is one of the better ways to explore the museum as they are very informative and free. The English tours take place at 11:00 on Tuesdays, Thursdays and Saturdays and there is a French-language tour on Thursdays at 09:00 and 12:00. Conveniently, there is a covered walkway from the National Museum that takes visitors over the highway to the southern stretch of the Lake Gardens.

National Museum Kuala Lumpur
Opening Hours: Daily, 09:00 - 18:00, closed on Hari Raya Puasa and Hari Raya Haji
Address: Jalan Damansara 50566, Kuala Lumpur, Malaysia
Tel: +603-2267-1048

How to get there: Near Sentral Station, however, you have to figure out the best way to walk across the highway to get there from that stop

National Planetarium in Kuala Lumpur

The National Planetarium (Planetarium Negara KL) is dedicated to all things related to science and astronomy. It's a fun and educational place for kids to learn about the planet and universe. Set on a hill to the east of Lake Gardens, it is topped by a blue dome easily visible from nearby roads.

It may not be as high tech as the planetariums of New York or London standards, but it still merits a visit. The main entrance is evocative of a teleport chamber which leads into a series of halls containing two planetariums that have interactive exhibits (touch-screen interactive computers and hands-on experiments) plus a Space Theatre.

Cool Interactive Exhibits

If you are feeling adventurous give the Space Ball at National Planetarium a go: it is a human-sized gyroscopic device that spins volunteers around. However only try it if you have a cast-iron stomach. There is also an eerie UV-lit lift labelled the Galeri Pemandangan (Observation Gallery) that takes you up a minaret-like tower to the Viewing Gallery. You are provided with binoculars here and from this advantageous position you get the best views of the Lake Gardens and the rest of downtown.

Space Theatre

The Space Theatre shows short, wide-screen IMAX international science and space films and generic documentaries at regular intervals throughout the day: it even shows clips from famous movies like Star Wars. However, hands down, the best place in the National Planetarium is the Observatory Park with models of Chinese and Indian astronomy systems and you can see distant planets through a telescope.

National Planetarium Kuala Lumpur

Opening Hours: Tuesday Sunday 09:00 16:30
Location: 53, Jalan Perdana, Kuala Lumpur
Address: +603 2273 4303

National Science Centre in Kuala Lumpur

The National Science Centre is a crowd puller with its vivacious, educational and just-plain-fun, hands on science and technology exhibits. Shaped like a futuristic, green mosque topped off with a large dome, it is divided into several sections, with exhibits covering the gamut of scientific knowledge.

Also known as the Pusat Sains Negara, Malaysia's first overhead freshwater aquarium, filled with 32 species of local freshwater fish, greets you as you make your way to the main exhibits. Established in 1996, the best part of the National Science Centre is undoubtedly the hall where you can watch a science show beamed straight into the interior of the main dome.

The National Science Centre easily stands shoulder-to-shoulder with the Petrosains Discovery Centre in KLCC: it is only the complex's out-of-the-way location in Mont Kiara instead of the city centre that makes it second string. The museum has gone to great lengths to ensure that the content in the exhibits are thoroughly tourist-friendly with plenty of signage in English.

Catering to both kids and adults, other facilities at the National Science Centre include a cafeteria, multimedia library, lecture hall and multi-purpose hall.

National Science Centre
Opening Hours: 09:00 17:00 (closed on Friday)
Location: Pesiaran Bukit Kiara, Bukit Kiara, Kuala Lumpur
Tel: +603 2089 3400

National Textiles Museum Kuala Lumpur

Situated within Merdeka Square along Jalan Sultan Hishamuddin, the National Textiles Museum is hailed as one of the most significant heritage landmarks in Kuala Lumpur city centre. Open to the public in 2010, the museum showcases the process and technology of textiles, and houses exquisite collections of traditional apparel, accessories, and textiles in Malaysia in a beautiful Mughal-Islamic style heritage building. Designed by Arthur Charles Alfred Norman (who also contributed to the design of the iconic Sultan Abdul Samad Building and Cathedral of St. Mary), four distinctive galleries can be found within the two-storey National Textiles Museum.

Pohon Budi Gallery

The first section exhibits the origin of textiles from prehistoric times and development through trade, as well as the tools, materials and techniques of textile-making practised over years. Situated on the ground floor, displays include the hands-on processes of calendaring and gilding, gold thread embroidery, knitting, beading, and batik-painting. Traditional apparels such as embroidered shawls, Iban ceremonial cloth, songket (hand-woven silk with intricate gold or silver thread patterns, headgear, and beaded shoes are also displayed in this gallery.

Pelangi Gallery

True to its name, Pelangi Gallery is a colourful display of batik (fabric imprinted with patterns through the application of wax and dye) in Malaysia, housing extensive textile designs from the Chinese, Baba and Nyonya communities, as well as examples of ethnic Sarawakian and Sabahan prints.

Teluk Berantai Gallery

This gallery highlights the predominant motif in the making of Malay songket called teluk berantai (interlocking bays), which is made up of a scattering of individual flower designs that's stitched together into beautiful geometric patterns. Located on the top floor of the National Textile Museum, guests can also view collections of Malay and Indian textiles, gold thread embroidery, and various Malay heritage costumes.

Ratna Sari Gallery

The final gallery is a glittering display of jewellery and accessories that are made with diamond, gold, silver, copper, beads, and even plants. Showcasing the expertise of Malaysia's various ethnic groups, exhibits include chastity belts, headdresses, hair pins, pendants, brooches, beaded shoes, bracelets, anklets, pemeleh (dangling earrings), cucuk sanggul (hairpin), rings, weapons, necklaces. There's also a display of mannequins adorning traditional attire from the indigenous Iban, Murut, Mah Meri communities in Sabah and Sarawak.

A great place to learn about Malaysia's rich history and diverse textiles, admission to the National Textiles Museum is free of charge. The best way to get to the National Textile Museum is via LRT alight at the Masjid Jamek stop and the museum is a mere eight-minute walk away. Alternatively, there are plenty of tours in KL that charter visitors to the Independence Square so make sure you don't miss the chance to visit!

Kuala Lumpur, Malaysia

National Textiles Museum Kuala Lumpur
Opening Hours: Daily 09:00 18:00
MRT: Masjid Jamek
Address: 26, Jalan Sultan Hishamuddin, Kuala Lumpur
Tel: +603 2694 3457 or +603 2694 346

National Visual Arts Gallery in Kuala Lumpur

National Visual Arts Gallery is flanked by the National Theatre and the National Library. A tranquil complex also known as the Balai Seni Visual Negara, it showcases a permanent collection of over 2,500 local and foreign works of art (including photography) by celebrated contemporary artists.

Locals refer to it simply as the National Art Gallery. The RM40 million complex is spread out over three floors and has seven galleries plus outdoor exhibition areas and a café. Established by the Majlis Kesenian Persekututan (Malay Arts Council) in 1958, it is the country's official venue for art workshops and exhibitions and even organises art classes for kids.

Design of Natonal Visual Arts Gallery
The National Visual Arts Gallery's architecture is similar to the Istana Budaya (National Theatre) next door: it is a blend of slate, tinted glass and clean modern lines with traditional Malay design prominent in the form of a light blue origami-style metallic roof. There is a pretty fountain just outside the main entrance.

The interior of the National Visual Arts Gallery has polished wooden floors and warm lighting and there is swirly Guggenheim Museum-style staircase that dominates the space.

Prominent Exhibits
A favourite piece at the National Visual Arts Gallery is a striking mural entitled, Graffiti, by Mahadir Masri by the walkway leading up to the main entrance of the gallery. Other noteworthy works of art include paintings by Zulkifli Moh'd Dohalan, Wong Hoi Cheong, Ahad Osman and the renowned batik artist Chuah Than Teng. Also showcased is a collection of 1900s

ceramics, a superb 1964 Chinese ink painting and a variety of other prints, photos, sculptures and textiles.

Exhibits at the National Visual Arts Gallery display the artist's name and the date of the piece but other information is unavailable.

Focus On Malaysia

The ground floor of the National Visual Arts Gallery is given over to temporary exhibitions of paintings, sculptures or photography that are primarily Malaysian (but also of other Southeast Asian countries). The second and third floors of the exhibit house the museum's permanent collection: you will find more contemporary canvases on the second floor colourful works of art with elements of Islamic design. The top floor sees the museum's more traditional works. Chiefly pieces focused on landscapes and portraits, these works have aspects of historical and rural Malaysia (think handicraft-making and music-playing) as its theme.

National Visual Arts Gallery

Opening Hours: 10:00 18:00
Address: 2, Jalan Temerloh, Off Jalan Tun Razak,
53200 Kuala Lumpur, Malaysia.
Tel: +603 4025 4990

Kuala Lumpur Zoo, Pandas & Aquarium

Kuala Lumpur Zoo and Aquarium, spanning over 110 acres around a central lake, houses 5137 specimens from 476 species of mammals, birds, reptiles, amphibians and fish from Asia and Africa. Also known as the Zoo Negara Malaysia, the wildlife sanctuary is located 13km northeast of Kuala Lumpur beyond Jalan Tun Razak along Jalan Ulu Klang. Housing a forest, lake and 16 animal exhibits, the zoo is set on such vast grounds that visitors will need at least three hours to explore in its entirety. To make it easier for foreign visitors to explore the zoo, tram rides are available for a surcharge of RM8 for adults and RM6 for children, while local visitors are charged at RM5 and RM3 respectively.

Some of Kuala Lumpur Zoo and Aquarium's most popular sections include the Reptile Park which features an exceptional collection of snakes, including the Sumatran pit viper and the Indian rock python, Malaysian Elephants exhibit, and Lake Birds which displays 300 free-roaming birds, while visitors can see leopard cats, capybara, slow lories, Malay civet, pumas, leopards, raccoons, striped hyenas and Binturong in the Mammal Kingdom exhibit. Housing wild animals from most parts of the world, the open-concept Ape Centre enclosure houses Sumatran orang-utans, while the Australian Plain exhibit is home to a group of wallabies, emus (Australia's largest bird), kangaroos, and pademelons: the smallest of the marsupials.

Situated within the zoo is the Tunku Abdul Rahman Aquarium, one of Malaysia's oldest and most extensive public aquariums. Housing a variety of common and endangered aquatic species, the aquarium is divided into several exhibits that emulate the natural environments found in Malaysia, including Peat Swamp Zone, the Mangrove Zone, and Marine Zone.

Kuala Lumpur Zoo and Aquarium also offers a kid-friendly exhibit called Children's World, where little ones can get up close and personal with rabbits, ducks, chickens, parrots and guinea pigs. The section also houses a mini-rainforest with a variety of plants, a small aviary, fish pond, miniature horse barn, playground, and a mini cave where numerous artefacts such as skulls of primates, and body parts of various animals can be found.

Pandas at Kuala Lumpur Zoo
The latest wildlife additions to Kuala Lumpur Zoo and Aquarium are two rare giant pandas hailing from Sichuan, China. Visitors are able to catch a glimpse of these highly endangered creatures behind a massive glass panel. Promising a fulfilling day with the entire family, visitors are treated to exciting animal shows held daily at 11:00 and 15:00, photo booths on

weekends, as well as guided tours, talks, seminars and interactive sessions.

Kuala Lumpur Zoo and Aquarium is accessible via a number of public transportation options. From Kuala Lumpur city centre, visitors can hail a taxi or hop on the Metrobus #16 from Central Market in Chinatown that takes them directly to the zoo.

Price Range: RM85 for adults (RM63 for ASEAN visitors) & RM43 for children 3 - 12 years old (RM33 for ASEAN)

National Zoo Kuala Lumpur
Opening Hours: 09:00 17:00
Location: Ulu Klang, Taman Melawati
Tel: +603 4108 3422

Perdana Botanical Garden in Kuala Lumpur

The Perdana Botanical Gardens, set within the Tun Abdul Razak Heritage Park, contain the largest collection of flower gardens and animal parks in Kuala Lumpur city centre. Also called Lake Gardens, this centrally-located recreational park is best visited during the weekends, when it's packed with locals enjoying various activities on the main square as well as along its many lakefront trails and landscaped hills.

One of its standout features is the Orchid Garden, which is a five-minute walk from the Kuala Lumpur Bird Park. This flower garden spans 10,000 square metres, housing walking paths and manmade fountains, as well as a semi-circle pergola and rock garden that house 800 species of orchids from both climbing and terrestrial varieties.

Another prominent attraction within the Perdana Botanical Gardens, Hibiscus Garden is where you can find Malaysia's national flower in full bloom. Less than 10 minutes away from the Kuala Lumpur Butterfly Park, this landscaped garden also houses a colonial-era building, where you can find a quaint tearoom and a gallery showcasing the history and significance of the hibiscus flower in Malaysian history.

Laman Perdana is located in the between both gardens, where you can find various events taking place at the main square. Located close to a manmade lake, the square is fitted with a massive semi-transparent awning, cafes serving light snacks and beverages, as well as gazebos overlooking the gardens

Open daily between 09:00 and 18:00, entrance to the Perdana Botanical Gardens is free all year long, though visiting the Orchid Garden and Hibiscus Garden requires a payment of RM1 on weekends. There are also additional entrance fees for some attractions within the park, including the bird and butterfly parks.

Aside from the gardens, the Perdana Botanical Gardens are highly frequented due to their proximity to some of KL's most notable landmarks, including the Islamic Arts Museum Malaysia, the National Monument, and the National Planetarium. Visitors can enjoy a tour of all the attractions within the Heritage Park via shuttle trams between 09:00 and 18:00, with tickets priced at RM6 for adults and RM2 for children.

Perdana Botanical Gardens
Opening Hours: Daily 07:00 20:00
Location: Jalan Kebun Bunga, Tasik Perdana, Kuala Lumpur
Tel: +603 2617 6404

Petronas Art Gallery in Kuala Lumpur

PETRONAS Art Gallery is also known as Galeri PETRONAS. It has over 1,000 local and international, traditional and contemporary works of art ranging from paintings and photographs to costumes and crafts. It is an easy place to find as it is located within the Suria KLCC shopping mall.

The PETRONAS Art Gallery is an understated yet elegant and brightly-lit gallery and was established in 1993 to support the development of art in the country. The non-profit gallery has a programme of changing art, craft and design exhibitions so each visit to the gallery is a unique experience. It used to be located in the Dayabumi Complex but moved to its present location in 1998.

Kuala Lumpur, Malaysia

PETRONAS Art Gallery
Opening Hours: Tuesday Sunday 10:00 20:00
Address: Lot 341-343, Level 3, Suria KLCC Kuala Lumpur, Kuala Lumpur City Centre
Tel: +603 2051 7770

Petronas Twin Towers in Kuala Lumpur

Petronas Twin Towers were once the tallest buildings in the world. Now the world's tallest twin structures, the 88-storey buildings were designed by Cesar Pelli & Associates with both towers joined at the 41st and 42nd floors (175m above street level) by a 58 metre-long, double-decker Sky Bridge.

Standing 452 metres tall, the Petronas Twin Towers retained its world-title claim to fame until 2004 when Taipei's 101 was built, measuring 508 metres tall. Today, the Burj Khalifa in Dubai (opened in 2010) retains the spot as the world's tallest building. Located in the KL city centre, the Petronas Twin Towers' architecture is Islamic-inspired and the buildings primarily house the corporate headquarters of the Petronas Company and other offices.

When the Petronas Twin Towers were completed in 1998 they were declared the tallest buildings in the world, surpassing the 442-metre-tall Willis Tower in Chicago, U.S.A. At the base of the Petronas Twin Towers is Suria KLCC, an upmarket shopping mall that is very popular with tourists.

Tower One is fully occupied by the Malaysian state oil company Petronas, and its subsidiaries and associate companies. Tower Two is mostly taken up by multinational companies such as Accenture, Al-Jazeera, Barclays Capital, Bloomberg, Boeing, IBM, McKinsey & Co., Microsoft, Reuters and more.

Fun for Everyone
Stretching out to the side of the Petronas Twin Towers is the spacious and beautifully landscaped KLCC Park which features a jogging track, walking paths, a water fountain and a wading pool for children.

Besides the mall and park, the Petronas Twin Towers has a host of other attractions including the Petronas Art Gallery and Kuala Lumpur Convention Centre. Plus the Petrosains Science Centre is here set inside Suria KLCC: it is an interactive science discovery centre showcasing exhibits related to the petroleum industry, from petroleum's origin in the age of the dinosaurs to its latest oil-based products.

Classical Tour de force

Another one of the Petronas Twin Towers' most notable features is the Dewan Filharmonik Petronas concert hall, Southeast Asia's leading venue for classical music. Located in between the two towers, the architectural design of the facility, which has earned praise as one of the world's best concert halls, is based upon the time-honoured design of 19th century European concert halls. The concert hall has played host to some of the world's most respected musical talents and is home to the Malaysian Philharmonic Orchestra.

A View from Above

Set on Level 86 is Petronas Twin Towers' observation deck, where visitors can get a closeup view of the tower's spire as well as digital displays and exhibit of the tower's history.

The double-decked Skybridge at the Petronas Twin Towers is one of its major draws as it offers amazing views of the city. Apart from allowing tenants of the towers to move from one building to the other without having to go to ground level, the Skybridge also functions as an emergency exit route.

Do note a pass is required to enter the bridge, so make sure to get there early as queues can be long.

Opening Hours: 09:00 19:00 (closed for Friday prayers 13:00 14:30)
Location: Near Concorde Hotel Monorail stop, in between Jalan Ampang and Jalan Raja Chulan
Petronas Twin Towers
Address: KLCC
How to get there: You can take the LRT and stop at the KLCC station.

Petrosains in Kuala Lumpur

Petrosains Kuala Lumpur is a 7,000sqm interactive science discovery centre located on the fourth floor of the Petronas Twin Towers. Good for a few hours of fun-filled activity, the complex is largely dedicated to the field of petroleum science and presents science and technology in a fun and entertaining way.

Arranged in an easy-to-navigate 'museum-style' concept with a collection of everything from space age exhibits to fossils, it is also a great place to learn more about other scientific issues. Since its opening in 1999, this hands-on interactive science museum has been popular with locals as well as expatriate families. Petrosains Kuala Lumpur is divided into 11 main interactive showcases, which can be visited in any order.

Petroleum Information

Petrosains Kuala Lumpur is arranged in a very straightforward manner and there's an underlying futuristic theme in most rooms. Explaining the petroleum industry in intriguing style, the gallery has placards with information for each exhibit. Those who fear that the facts might be too complicated need not worry it may be worded in a complex way but that doesn't mean it'll be over your head.

The main gallery starts out at the Lobby, where there is a soothing water sculpture and a Sauber PETRONAS Formula One racing car a shiny example of PETRONAS' involvement in the development of advanced engine technology and performance.

Exploration
Once you have purchased your ticket, it's time to discover the Exploration section here hi-tech tools and techniques used for petroleum exploration are displayed; it's the perfect place for budding geologists or seismologists to catch a glimpse of life on the job.

Next up is a visit to Speed, an area where Formula One (F1) fans can find hands-on exhibits on the science and technology behind the vehicles. Besides that, there's a mini theatre The Molecule Nano World that seats up to 32 people, which showcases 3D movies.

Dark Ride at Petrosains
Next up is the Dark Ride truly the beginning of your journey into Petrosains Kuala Lumpur. This 'ride' is shaped like an oil drop, and takes you through the tranquil rainforests of Malaysia, up mountains and diving into seas in an effort to show you Malaysia's transformation and its advancement into the new millennium. Meanwhile, the Sparkz zone has a 'grain pit', a little inventor's section and an interactive art display at Tot Spot. Beginning at the Molecule Stairway, the Molecule Nano World takes visitors around exhibits in the 'nano' world of atoms and molecules; its basically chemistry-type attractions and displays with kitschy but cute 'guides' Moly and Poly.

Petrojaya
The next section is Petrojaya, a 'village' with cartoon-oriented exhibits introducing the effects that petrochemicals play in local daily life this display

intersperses dynamic high technology with the Malaysian art of wayang kulit (shadow play) to create a unique showcase. Another attraction in the same vein is the Geotime Diorama this exhibit takes you back about 200 million years, with a 'singing' dinosaur and also showcases of earthquakes, fossils and petroleum. One of Petrosains Kuala Lumpur's last displays is the Music and Art zone a showcase that seamlessly blends music and art into the field of science and last but not least, is the Exit Ride a parting journey that presents some of Malaysia's greatest achievements projected in an audio visual display, ending beneath a star-studded 'sky'.

It's easy to see why Petrosains Kuala Lumpur is busy on a regular basis it's not a simplified tourist attraction but it still presents lots of information in a fun and entertaining way, and what's more, there are two IMAX 3D cinemas and an iWerks theatre here. Weekends are crowded so the best time to visit Petrosains is on weekdays in the late afternoons, when the school excursions are over. Visitors who aren't captivated by the exhibits shouldn't spend too much time trying to find meaning in the museum rather, enjoy it for what it is: a tribute to the petroleum science industry.

Petrosains Kuala Lumpur
Opening Hours: Tuesday - Friday 09:30 - 17:30,
Saturday & Sunday 09:30 - 18:30
Address: Level 4, Suria KLCC, PETRONAS Twin Towers, Kuala Lumpur City Centre
Tel: +603 2331 8181

Putra World Trade Centre in Kuala Lumpur

Putra World Trade Centre is an international convention and trade fair location. Also known as Pusat Dagangan Dunia Putra, the 42-storey complex spans across 1.7 million sqft. The US$10 million complex was constructed in 1981 and it is located to the north of the city centre on Jalan Tun Ismail.

A popular spot for some of the country's major exhibitions, Malaysia is justifiably proud of it. The luxurious complex of buildings includes the Pan-Pacific Hotel, a sleek 41-storey office block and a 253,000sqft exhibition centre (with four halls) topped with a Minangkabau-style roof. The top floor of this luxurious centre is home to the UMNO (United Malays National Organisation) offices, former Prime Minister Dr. Mahatir Mohamad's ruling party.

Good to Know
second floor. In the past, major international events such as the PATA General Conference (1986), CHOGM Head of State Meeting (1989) and NAM General Conference (2003) been held at Putra World Trade Centre.

The complex is easily accessible via taxi; alternatively, the PWTC Ampang Line LRT station is just a short walk away.

Putra World Trade Centre
Address: 41, Jalan Tun Ismail, KL

Kuala Lumpur, Malaysia

Tel: +603 2614 6999

Royal Malaysian Police Museum

The Royal Malaysian Police Museum in Kuala Lumpur is a an offbeat yet interesting gem, especially for those keen to learn more about the work and history of Malaysian police. Situated in Jalan Perdana, the museum is in the cluster of the city's most famous attractions the Planetarium and Islamic Arts Museum are within the vicinity although if you're not careful, you might drive just right past it! Previously an archive of criminal evidence for police trainees' references, the museum has been revamped to accommodate more exhibits, and has been relocated to its current spot from its previous one at Police Training Centre in Jalan Semarak.

Sporting a slightly traditional look, with its arrow-shaped wooden structure, the museum encompasses three galleries, aptly named 'A', 'B' and 'C'. Gallery A takes you through the history of the formation of the police squad in Malaysia, from the days of Federated and Unfederated Malay States to the current country structure, in a form of exhibits of official police uniforms and traditional weaponry such as kris (prized asymmetrical daggers) and cannons. Those who are interested in the early days of the Malacca Sultanate empire can also learn about its history and downfall, through paintings, drawings and weaponry displays.

Gallery B focuses more on the official vehicles and evidence of kept by the Royal Malaysian Police squad. Notable exhibits include confiscated weapons of triads and secret societies that used to wreck havoc in the country, with highlights being handmade gadgets from the Botak Chin clan that used to conduct armed robberies back in 1970's. Gallery C meanwhile offers a more in-depth explanation of the role of the police during several catastrophes in Malaya, namely the Japanese Occupation period and the infamous Bukit Kepong tragedy, a 1950 armed encounter between the

Kuala Lumpur, Malaysia

Federation of Malaya Police and Malaya Communist Party

More of the Royal Malaysian Police Squad achievements and ratings, such as awards and badges are also exhibited, with lists of names of its recipients. The Royal Malaysian Police squad is also known to be very active in sports, and displays profiles of the athletes who are also policemen. Entrance to the museum is free, and photography is prohibited in the museum grounds.

The Jalan Perdana strip houses some of the nation's best attractions, such as the KL Bird Park, the Islamic Arts Museum and National Mosque. To get to the museum, disembark at the nearest KTM Komuter station, Kuala Lumpur, and it shouldn't take more than a ten-minute walk to reach it.

Royal Malaysian Police Museum
Opening Hours: Tuesday Sunday 10:00 18:00; Friday 10:00 12:30, 14:30 18:00
Address: 5, Jalan Perdana, Kuala Lumpur

Tel: +6 03 2272 5689 / +6 03 2272 5690 / +6 03 2273 4740
Price Range: Free (weekdays); RM1 (weekends, public holidays)

Royal Selangor Visitor's Centre

An interactive exhibit of pewter manufacturing, the Royal Selangor Visitor's Centre is a 40,000sqft attraction housing a series of galleries, a factory and retail store. Recognised as one of the country's premier tourist attractions, the place receives between 800 and 1,200 guests daily. Living up to its royal title, the air-conditioned, glass-sided building is gorgeous (think water fountains, warm lighting and polished wooden floors) and well-managed, with free guided tours in several languages (English, Malay, Mandarin, Cantonese and Japanese) provided.

One sunny weekday afternoon the Royal Selangor Visitor's Centre beckons and we make a road trip of it, travelling more than 45 minutes outside of the city to visit the gallery and factory. For those concerned about the distance, worry not because the centre provides a free shuttle service to and from several KL hotels, making it super easy to visit.

A pliable metal alloy composed of copper and tin, pewter is much favoured for the manufacturing of 'silverware' (such as teapots, photo frames and even jewellery) due to its low melting point of 230° centigrade. Easily shaped by hand and machine tools, this bright material is certainly catchy to look at, with Kuala Lumpur being home to Royal Selangor, one of the world's largest pewter manufacturers. Set up in 1885 by a pewter smith from China, today the Royal Selangor brand has stores in most major KL malls, plus a visitor's centre (the Royal Selangor Visitor's Centre) in Setapak Jaya, the first in Asia and one of only three in the world.

In the gallery section of the Royal Selangor Visitor's Centre you can find showcases displaying aspects of pewter craftsmanship, from the science and history of it, to its unique qualities and fantastic applications.

Meanwhile, the factory (with over 250 skilled craftsmen hard at work) showcases the metalworking process, while the retail store houses the final product ranging from pewter merchandise to silver and gold jewellery.

We love the fact that the Royal Selangor Visitor's Centre has a really hands-on approach there are sections where you can see, hear and touch pewter products and even one area where you can try 'working' the metal. For example, while visiting the factory we are given a task to 'knock' circular patterns onto a pewter mug! It sounds easy, but let's just say it was anything but no wonder the craftsmen at Royal Selangor train for many years before they are cleared to work!

One of our favourite exhibits is the Chamber of Chimes, a space dedicated to demonstrating the difference between the resonant sound of cast pewter and that of similar metallic and organic materials. We had lots of silly fun going back and forth among the chimes.

Some of the highlights at the Royal Selangor Pewter Centre include the world's largest tankard (6ft 6 in, 3,432lbs), awarded by the Guinness Book of Records in 1987. We are also impressed with the 9.1m (over two-storey high) replica of the PETRONAS Twin Towers, made from 7,062 Royal Selangor pewter tankards.

Entry to Royal Selangor Visitor's Centre is free but if you are looking to get some hands-on experience with pewter making, we suggest a pit stop at the School of Hard Knocks or The Foundry. You will have to pay to take part in the workshops but you will get to take your creations home with you, plus a certificate for taking part

At the School of Hard Knocks, the project is standardised as you will be making a pewter bowl with your name engraved on the inside, using the same tools that were used over 100 years ago. The process takes over an hour and the workshop is a great place for groups and even kids!

Meanwhile, The Foundry is for those with a little more creative spirit what you make in this tiny room is really up to you. They have casts for pendants and key chains but let your imagination run away from you and create quirky pewter products you won't find anywhere else we made dog tags, stamped with our name, rank (job title) and serial numbers (date). One thing is for certain it was a super fun and memorable outing to the Royal Selangor Visitor's Centre!

Lastly, don't forget to take a stroll through the retail store on the ground floor even if you are not in shopping mode, it is worth it, just to see some of the intricate and gorgeous pewter pieces.

Royal Selangor Visitor's Centre
Opening Hours: 09:00 17:00
Address: No. 4 Jalan Usahawan 6, 53300 Setapak Jaya, Kuala Lumpur
Tel: +603 4145 6233

Rumah Penghulu Abu Seman

Kuala Lumpur, Malaysia

Rumah Penghulu Abu Seman is a meticulously-restored Malay house that is the highlight of a trip to Badan Warisan Malaysia (The Heritage Trust) in Kuala Lumpur. The house offers visitors a fascinating look back into the traditional way of life of Malaysians, and the story of the house is interesting in its own right.

Built between 1910 and 1930, this headman's residence was originally located in Kampung Sungai Kechil, which is a small village in Mukim Bagan Samak, Kedah. It was then moved to KL by the Heritage of Malaysia Trust as part of its ongoing efforts in the preservation and conservation of the country's architectural heritage

The stilted, wooden house was owned by Penghulu Abu Seman bin Nayan, who was the village headman in the state of Kedah. A series of constructions were conducted from the mid 1920s to the early 1930s and after his passing, his son Ibrahim bin Abu Seman inherited both the title and the ownership of the house. As Penghulu Ibrahim passed on without a successor of his own, the house was eventually left vacant until the Heritage of Malaysia Trust purchased it from Ibrahim's heir. In 1996, Rumah Penghulu Abu Seman was carefully disassembled and relocated to the Badan Warisan Malaysia Heritage Centre in Jalan Stonor.

Elevated by stilts, the all-black exterior stands out against its garden-like surroundings. Inside, the beautiful living quarters seem to be frozen in time as it is adorned with artefacts and furniture from the early 1900s. Within the property's grounds is the Heritage Garden, which houses a selection of herbs and plants that are indigenous to Malaysia.

While you can wander around Rumah Penghulu Abu Seman at your own pace, there are also guided tours where you can learn more about the history of the house. Available from Mondays to Saturdays at 11:00 and 15:00, the tour is priced at a minimum of RM10 per person, which is used for maintenance and upkeep of the house. Situated within Kuala Lumpur city centre,

Rumah Penghulu Abu Seman is accessible within a 15-minute walk from the Bukit Bintang monorail station.

Rumah Penghulu Abu Seman
Opening Hours: Tuesday Saturday 10:00 16:00
Address: 2 Jalan Stonor, Kuala Lumpur
Tel: +603 2144 9273
Price Range: Tour - RM10

Sky Box at Sky Deck KL Tower

Sky Box at Sky Deck KL Tower, standing at 300 metres above ground, offers visitors a vertigo-inducing view of Kuala Lumpur. Similar to Melbourne's Eureka Skydeck 88, this fully-transparent viewing box extends out from the Sky Deck ledge and can accommodate up to six people at a time, allowing for plenty of room for photo-snapping with a backdrop of the city skyline.

Entrance to the Sky Box is included in the tickets for Observation Deck at KL Tower, which cost RM105 for adults and RM55 for children, while those with a valid MyKad pay only RM75 and RM39 respectively. Although a time limitation isn't imposed, do be considerate of other visitors and not linger too long in the Sky Box.

After visiting the Sky Box at Sky Deck KL Tower, make your way to Atmosphere 360, a revolving restaurant that's known for its array of western and local cuisine, elegant décor and furnishing, as well as floor-to-ceiling windows overlooking Kuala Lumpur. Aside from the observation deck, Menara KL Tower is surrounded by numerous attractions for families, including a mini zoo, the KL Eco Forest Park, XD Theatre (with a 6D motion simulated thrill ride), aquarium, and an upside-down house

Sky Box at Sky Deck KL Tower
Opening Hours: Daily 10:00 22:00
Address: KL Tower, Jalan P. Ramlee, Kuala Lumpur
Tel: +603 2020 5444

Sri Kandaswamy Kovil Hindu Temple

Sri Kandaswamy Kovil Hindu Temple is a colourful, ornate shrine dedicated to the Hindu deity Lord Muruga. A popular tourist attraction that dates to

1902, it is centrally located along Lorong Scott inn Brickfields, about a 10-minute drive from KL Sentral Station and the Little India commercial district.

Featuring a traditional Sri Lankan architectural style, the entrance is decorated with statues of hundreds of Hindu deities. Local devotees believe this shrine to be the threshold between the material and spiritual worlds. Sri Kondaswamy Kovil Hindu Temple houses a pavilion beside a reflecting lotus pond, with peacocks wandering through the main courtyard. Photography is not allowed inside the house of worship, but you can take photos of its colourful entrance gate

Sri Kandaswamy Kovil Hindu Temple is best visited during annual festivities such as Thaipusam (January or February), when you get to see thousands of devotees offering prayers to the statue of Lord Muruga before making their way to the iconic Batu Caves. On this occasion, devotees walk about 15 kilometres to the temple caves while carrying silver pots filled with milk, flowers, and various gifts above their heads.

Open daily, entrance to the temple is free of charge. As with any religious site in Malaysia, do dress appropriately and refrain from disturbing the monks and devotees during your visit in Sri Kondaswamy Kovil Hindu Temple

Sri Kandaswamy Kovil Hindu Temple
Opening Hours: Daily 05:30 –13:00 & 17:00 21:30
Address: 3, Lorong Scott, Brickfields, Kuala Lumpur
Tel: +603 2274 2987

Nightlife

Kuala Lumpur is a vibrant and lively nocturnal hub of countless bars, pubs and clubs on the streets, as well as swanky rooftop establishments situated within five-star hotels. From Bangsar's cocktail bars to Changkat Bukit Bintang's chic see-and-be-seen nightclubs spinning hip-hop and house tracks, it's safe to say that there's no shortage of exciting places to go at night in Kuala Lumpur.

KL nightlife is packed with a diverse range of party goers - from local youths and expats to international travellers. By 22:00, the nightlife scene in Kuala Lumpur comes alive, with nightspots offering a winning combination of lively and friendly ambience, extensive alcoholic offerings, and talented DJs spinning dance-worthy tunes until the wee hours of morning.

Nightlife experiences in Kuala Lumpur are plentiful as the city is teeming with bars, pubs and clubs on the streets, and swanky rooftop restaurants and bars situated within five-star hotels. After the sun sets, the city becomes alive with nightspots offering a winning combination of lively and friendly ambience, extensive alcoholic beverages, and talented DJs spinning dance-worthy tunes.

However, nightlife in KL isn't just limited to watering holes as you can also find numerous hawker stalls with tantalising Asian cuisine and bustling night markets that remain open until the wee hours of the morning. From Jalan Alor's bustling hawker stalls and seafood restaurants to Changkat Bukit Bintang's chic see-and-be-seen nightclubs spinning hip-hop and house tracks, this comprehensive guide of 10 Best Nightlife Experiences in Kuala Lumpur shows that there's no shortage of exciting places to go at night in Kuala Lumpur.

Changkat Bukit Bintang Nightlife

All the rage in Kuala Lumpur now, Changkat Bukit Bintang nightlife is well-regarded as the 'it' party venue in the city's lively yet fluid clubbing scene. A busy street that's lined with plenty of international two-storey restobars, snazzy nightclubs, posh cocktail lounges, subdued whisky bars, and lively Irish pubs, it is one of the city's most vibrant boulevards.

Hosting plenty of themed nights, international DJs, and live band performances, it's safe to say that nightlife in Changkat Bukit Bintang is anything but dull. Amongst the bevy of watering holes available here, there are a few establishments that stand out due to their unique concepts. Stand-up comedy, gay friendly parties, foreign film screenings and open mic nights are just some of the events you can find on Changkat Bukit Bintang.

Bonne Gilla Bar & Restaurant
Bonne Gilla Bar & Restaurant is known for its pork dishes served in generous portions, but diners can also find a selection of pastas, seafood, lamb and poultry on the menu. Tucked away from the vibrant Changkat Bukit Bintang in KL City Centre, it also boasts an extensive and affordable wine list you can enjoy house wines like Australian Sauvignon Blanc and Chilean Chardonnay for RM110 by the bottle and RM17 by the glass. Bottled wines cost less than RM200, with imports from France, Argentina, Australia and New Zealand.

Opening Hours: Mon Thu & Sun 15:00 02:00, Fri & Sat 15:00 03:00
Address: 31 Jalan Berangan, Changkat Bukit Bintang, Kuala Lumpur
Tel: +6016 365 6113

Brix Union Gastro Pub
Brix Union Gastro Pub is fitted with plenty of TV screens that attract sports lovers looking to catch the

latest live sports, while its extensive menu of hearty burgers, pastas, pork ribs and alcoholic offerings makes it a must-visit when you're in need of some comfort food. Located along Jalan Changkat Bukit Bintang, this English-inspired pub also offers attractive all-day promos like RM165 for a tower of Carlsberg, shisha and a pan pizza. Great for sharing, a bucket of five Asahi, Tiger and Somersby here costs RM100.

Opening Hours: Daily 15:00 - 03:00
Address: 51, Jalan Changkat Bukit Bintang, Kuala Lumpur
Tel: +603 2145 7100

Ceylon Bar
One of the longest running bars in Changkat Bukit Bintang, Ceylon Bar draws a steady clientele of expats and locals due to its relaxed vibe and friendly staff. Adorned with kitschy decor and impressive beverage offerings, guests can opt to order a drink at the terrace upstairs or unwind by the bar and immerse themselves in football matches aired on the bar's flat screen television. Ceylon Bar also offers mouth-watering Sri

Lankan and western fare in massive portions such as savoury BBQ pork ribs and fried rice platter with plenty of chicken, fish cakes, eggs, and prawn crackers. Delicious cocktails are offered in this establishment as well, namely Ceylon Island Iced Tea, frozen margarita, and snowball (advocaat liquor, and sprite).

Opening Hours: Monday Saturday 17:00 01:00,
Sunday 11:00 01:00; Closed on Tuesdays
Address: 20-2 Changkat Bukit Bintang
Tel: +603 2145 7689

Fire and Ice Club
Fire and Ice Club is a vibrant nightlife venue along Jalan Changkat Bukit Bintang, with a bar (and live bands from Tuesday to Sunday) on the ground floor and a spacious nightclub upstairs. Every Wednesday, resident DJs spin R&B and hip hop tunes until late while ladies get to enjoy free chocolate martinis, Long Island iced teas, tequila or Sex on the Beach from 21:00 onwards. The club also offers attractive promos for the opposite sex on Thursdays, including two-for-one on draught beers, house wines, cocktails and shooters until 23:00.

Opening Hours: Daily 15:00 - 03:00
Address: 24, Jalan Changkat Bukit Bintang, Kuala Lumpur
Tel: +6017 632 4961

Fuzio Bar & Ristorante
Offering Italian cuisine in a classy setting, Fuzio Bar & Ristorante is a two-storey restaurant situated just a few lots after Bakita in Jalan Berangan. Pastas and pizzas feature heavily on its menu, along with main courses of grilled lamb rack, baked cod fish, and beef tenderloin; but the restaurant also serves a noteworthy dish of grilled rabbit and rabbit ragout. Cocktails, mocktails, whisky and various liquors are served for fun-filled gatherings with friends while a wine cellar boasting French labels pairs well with meat dishes. Invoking a fine-dining environment, Fuzio Bar & Ristorante is decorated with oak furnishings, warm lighting, and neutral earth tones. While the ground floor caters to a large group with long tables and spacious seats, the second floor is best for diners who prefer a candlelit dinner in an intimate setting. Fuzio

Bar & Ristorante is a non-smoking establishment but diners can head to the rooftop lounge for a livelier nocturnal concept.

Opening Hours: Monday Saturday 17:00 01:00
Address: 29, Jalan Berangan, Kuala Lumpur
Tel: +603 2110 0303

Hubba Bar at Invito Hotel Suites
Hubba Bar, situated on the ground floor of Invito Hotel Suites, is a quirky cafe by day and a vibrant drinking joint by night. Just a five-minute walk from the ever-bustling Changkat Bukit Bintang, its spacious interior is decorated with an eclectic mix of bicycle installations, wooden furnishings, hanging vines, and quirky cartoons painted on the exposed walls. Great for a fun evening with friends, Hubba Bar's alcohol-infused desserts such as the Bailey's Chendol (coconut ice cream, red bean, cendol, palm sugar syrup and Bailey's Irish Cream) are simply delectable. For drinks, Hubba Bar serves a decent selection of bottled beers, imported wines, as well as classic and signature cocktails.

Opening Hours: Daily 07:00 02:00
Address: Ground Floor, Invito Hotel Suites, 1, Lorong Ceylon, Kuala Lumpur
Tel: +6017 786 7611

Reggae Bar
Reggae Bar, re-located to Zion Club, is one of the oldest surviving bars in Changkat Bukit Bintang. Offering a chilled-out vibe with a Jamaican theme, the bar is decked out in a colour scheme of red, yellow and green with a massive bar downstairs and a balcony area upstairs. Reggae Bar mostly caters for the western palate and features Italian pastas, pizzas, salads, meat cuts like fillet steak and lamb racks and even fish and chips. A satisfying selection of beverages including wine, cocktails, local and international beers are offered here as well. With a wonderful ambience unlike other bars in Changkat Bukit Bintang, Reggae Bar is a perfect good choice for an exciting night out or even a place to unwind during the weekend.

Opening Hours: Daily 16:00 03:00
Address: 31, Changkat Bukit Bintang, Kuala Lumpur
Tel: +603 2141 8163

Table 23 Kuala Lumpur

Table 23 is a quaint bar and restaurant in Jalan Mesui, a modest yet vibrant alternative to the often overcrowded Changkat Bukit Bintang. Adopting a rustic theme with exposed brick walls, unpolished wooden tables, hanging filament light bulbs, and a spacious al fresco dining area, it is the perfect place for hosting any occasion, from intimate dinners to casual gatherings with a large group of friends.

Serving Asian cuisine by day and Western delicacies by night, Table 23's must-try dish is its beef cheek served with bacon, parmentier potatoes, cherry tomatoes and zucchini. Perfectly tender yet full of flavour, it is a sinfully meaty dish that pairs well with a glass of wine. In addition to its wide range of draught beers, wines, and cocktails, Table 23 also hosts a number of live performances with happy hour promos starting from 17:00 till 22:00.

Opening Hours: Monday - Friday 11:30 01:00,
Saturday 16:00 01:00
Address: 23, Jalan Mesui, Kuala Lumpur

Tel: +603 2857 1051

Great Rooftop Bars in KL

There's no doubt about it Kuala Lumpur is a vibrant, bustling city from sunrise to sunset. To gain a whole new appreciation for Malaysia's capital, we recommend you get away from the busy streets and take in the view from a whole new angle the rooftops.

Best of all, Kuala Lumpur is home to numerous nocturnal hotspots, ranging from classy ristorantes to cocktail lounges, that are nestled atop high-rise structures. Our 10 Great Rooftop Bars in Kuala Lumpur offer great ambience for those who want to sit back and watch the sun set below the city horizon - with a drink in hand, of course.

Marini's on 57 Kuala Lumpur

Marini's on 57 is an exclusive Italian ristorante set on the 57th floor of Petronas Tower 3. Located in the heart of the KL city centre, it consists of a restaurant, bar and lounge. In the private elevator the atmosphere is hushed, but when you pass through the front doors the feel turns into one of refined elegance with the sounds of champagne glasses clinking and quiet chatter.

The dining area décor is white with casual, modern furnishings: meanwhile, the bar has art deco furniture and neon lights, and the lounge has a Havana-esque feel with brown leather sofas in different sizes. Paintings from Italian artist, Rosalba Mangione hang on the walls, while floor-to-ceiling windows and a glass roof provide great views of KL.

Offering Italian food, the restaurant has à la carte options but we liked the specials that our server recommended, like the spaghetti with botargo (mullet roe) and almonds it had terrific texture and lots of flavour. Also good was the pan-fried sea bass stuffed with shrimp and lemon dressing a terrific, zesty dish. Portions are small but each dish has unforgettable taste.

The bar has an extensive selection of wines, but there are also great cocktails and champagnes. Meanwhile, the Lounge (looking very much like an exclusive gentleman's club) is for those who want to sip on their Highland Park, Yamakazi, Johnnie Walker Blue and Johnnie Walker Gold in style. Tavern-style shelves house a collection of bottles that include single cask whiskies from independent bottlers and special-edition scotches from big distilleries.

In the background an in-house deejay alternates between haunting, soul-searching smooth jazz, dance tunes and techno beats, but the music plays softly so you can converse easily.

Petronas Tower 3 is set adjacent to Suria KLCC: there is an elevator beside the Versace store in Suria KLCC shopping mall which links directly to Petronas Tower 3. Alternatively, from Mandarin Oriental hotel, turn right: from here you can see the Cartier store and Petronas Tower 3. There is a signboard for Marini's on 57 and a waiting attendant will hand you an access card for the private elevator.

Marini's on 57
Opening Hours: Monday - Thursday 15:00 - 01:30, Friday & Saturday 15:00 - 03:00 & Sunday 17:00 - 01:30
Address: Level 57, Menara 3 Petronas, Persiaran KLCC, Kuala Lumpur
Tel: +603 2386 6030 or +6017 688 0167

SkyBar at Traders Hotels in KL

Sky Bar is a glamorous cocktail lounge set on the 33rd floor of Traders Hotel KL. A local institution, this rooftop nightclub is quite possibly the coolest venue on KL's nightlife scene the place to see and be seen at. It is recommended not only for its good location and giddying views over the city, but also its excellent drinks.

Airy and sexy, the centrepiece at Sky Bar is a pool that is bordered by 'cabanas' (large sunken alcoves with chaise longues) on one side, and a bar area with sofas and woven rattan high tables and bar stools on the other.

We recommend you grab a cabana to make the most of the full height windows and get the best views of KL city. The panorama from the bar area is no less impressive a skylight overhead makes you feel like you are on top of the world, with KL's famous twin towers clearly visible.

Sky Bar has no theme or overplayed concept, but this industrial-chic bar has definite character and feels like a secret club with a refined, sultry vibe to it.

A must-visit if you are planning on hitting the nightclubs in KL, resident DJs spin techno music at Sky Bar on select nights. On other nights tunes alternate from jazz, easy listening and soft rock to modern pop hits, but it plays discreetly in the background, allowing for easy conversation.

Kuala Lumpur, Malaysia

From Jalan Bukit Bintang Traders Hotel KL is approximately two km away and the easiest way to get here is to take a ten-minute taxi ride.

Sky Bar has good food sure, it is mostly finger food, such as spice-crusted calamari and vegetable spring rolls, but these snacks come in generous portions. We recommend the tasty and stomach-filling buffalo inferno wings and crispy barbecue beef ribs.

Though there is a variety of wines, beers and spirits, the cocktails are the real stars here: we recommend the bar's signature drinks such as the tangy-tasting Selangor Sling or the sweet and fruity passion fruit-based Mata D' Or. The best night to visit is Monday and Tuesdays when Sky Bar has good deals during their Retro Happy Hour.

Sky Bar
Opening Hours: 10:00 01:00 Sunday Thursday; 10:00 03:00 Friday & Saturday
Address: Level 33, Traders Hotel Kuala Lumpur, Kuala Lumpur City Centre
Tel: +603 2332 9911

Luna Bar in Pacific Regency Suites

Luna Bar is a two-storey rooftop bar on the 34th floor of Pacific Regency Suites. One of the city's best-known nightclubs, it offers 360° views of the city, including fantastic vistas of the Petronas Twin Towers. The place is divided into an al fresco lounge with a swimming pool and long bar on the lower level, while the top deck is a trendy indoor restaurant that overlooks the pool.

Just like Sky Bar at Traders Hotel KL, there is no overplayed theme here: the lower level has simple dark wood rattan chairs and chaise longues with white cushions that surround the pool. Meanwhile, the top deck has polished concrete floors that pair up well with modern red-and-white sofas, standing tables by the bar and warm lighting that creates a sophisticated mood.

Luna Bar takes advantage of its sky-high location with discreet background music, allowing for easy conversation and giving the place a relaxed, intimate atmosphere. The dress code leans towards smart casual with people who come to see and be seen, but the vibe never gets too pretentious.

Luna Bar serves the usual variety of beers, wines and spirits but the cocktails are really one of the main reasons to come for we especially like Luna Bar's signature cocktail, the Luna. A mixture of dark rum, Cointreau, blue Curacao and lychee liqueur, the sweet and fruity drink was served with longan fruit and sago and tasted very refreshing.

The breezy Luna Bar is both a restaurant and bar: the food menu ranges from appetisers, salads and soups to a la carte mains that you can enjoy poolside or at the indoor lounge. The food is good value especially when you consider the club's rooftop location.

We recommend the hearty Luna mixed grill, a platter of tender beef tenderloin, succulent lamb cutlets, homemade sausage and prawns. Also good is the chicken liver parfait, served with delicious grilled bread and onion jam a unique and memorable dish.

Luna has a cover charge of RM50 after 23:30 during the weekends but then again, considering the view, great cocktails and tasty food, it is well worth it.

Combining the relaxed air of an outdoor bar and the sophistication of an indoor lounge, with excellent rooftop views, Luna Bar is undoubtedly one of the city's best nightclubs.

Located directly opposite Menara KL Tower, a stalwart on the city's tourist scene, it is pretty easy to get to Luna Bar simply hop on the monorail train to the Bukit Nanas station and take a 10-minute walk to Pacific Regency Hotel.

Luna Bar
Opening Hours: Monday - Thursday & Sunday 11:00 - 01:00, Friday & Saturday 11:00 - 03:00
Address: Pacific Regency Hotel Suites, Menara Pan Global, Jalan Punchak, off Jalan P Ramlee, Kuala Lumpur
Tel: +603 2332 7777

Troika Sky Dining at Kuala Lumpur

Troika Sky Dining can be described in one word - impressive. Kuala Lumpur locals are becoming spoilt for choice when it comes to fine dining restaurants with a view, but this venue certainly stands out from the pack. Set in Tower B of The Troika along Persiaran KLCC, it comprises two dining venues and a bar: fusion-focused Cantaloupe, Italian bistro Strato and Claret wine bar.

Popular with young, trendy urbanites, from the outside The Troika blends in with the rest of the city's industrial skyline, looking like just any other concrete, steel and glass structure. However, inside each of the building's dining and drinking venues is an entirely different experience with low-key yet stylish design schemes that allow the views to take centre stage.

Cantaloupe

Set on The Troika's 23rd floor, Cantaloupe is not really a rooftop establishment, but its floor-to-ceiling angled glass windows overlook the city and offer a weatherproof dining experience at an altitude. The kitchen is helmed by Chef Christian Bauer (formerly of Frangipani restaurant fame along Changkat Bukit Bintang), offering a concise, haute menu with French, Italian, Greek and Spanish flavours evident in its dishes.

We recommend you start off your three-course meal here with truffled poached egg (RM50) with savoury barley cream, Swiss chard, egg yolk foam, beef fat vinaigrette, crisp dried beef and truffle batonnet. Next, we recommend lamb tartare (RM75), hand chopped juicy lamb loin with soft egg yolk and tender smoky duck cooked in shallot oil with tangy garlic crisps and topped with crispy croutons and glazed figs. Follow up with the roast Wagyu sirloin (RM95) served with truffle potatoes, crunchy Brussels sprouts and sweet glazed carrots.

Strato

Head up the discreet spiral staircase, past craquelure paintwork and you will find Troika Sky Dining's Strato. The Italian bistro has mastered the art of being trendy yet welcoming, with industrial themed interior design think, cream loungers, marble-topped tables, wooden floors and steel fixtures setting the tone. Meanwhile, the menu is assertive and adventurous, taking pizzas and pastas to the next level: stalwarts like bolognaise and carbonara are available but they have been upgraded with the addition of high-end ingredients. We recommend the ravioli in sage butter (RM55), served with melt-in-your-mouth slices of Wagyu beef cheek and fried onions; also good is the juicy, over roasted chicken breast with basil and mozzarella (RM55). Fast and friendly service seals the deal.

Claret

Just across the room from Cantaloupe is Claret, a wine bar that also does a fine line in cocktails. The antithesis of a large impersonal drinking barn, the décor is understated and elegant with lots of wood and steel fixtures, and plenty of quirky furniture (like a blue velvet couch and hounds-tooth chairs) to add a cosy touch. Best of all, there is an outdoor terrace with Chesterfield sofas where you can take in a cool gin and tonic while admiring the ever-evolving skyline.

Expect a thoroughly sexy vibe at whichever site you choose, and it goes without saying that the cloud-skimming views will be something else: they also host a series of pretty worthwhile monthly wine tasting events. Whether you are here for business meetings, family dinner, or just networking, Troika Sky Dining certainly caters to all

Troika Sky Dining
Opening Hours: Daily 12:00 15:00 &18:00 23:00 (Strato), 16:00 01:00 (Claret), 18:30 22:30 (Cantaloupe Dining Room)
Address: Level 23A, Tower B, The Troika, 19 Persiaran KLCC, Kuala Lumpur
Tel: +603 2162 0886

Chinatown Kuala Lumpur Nightlife

Nightlife in Chinatown Kuala Lumpur is in a league of its own; it's not about rows of clubs, pubs and bars offering music-and-alcohol-fuelled entertainment, but the extra colour that seems to grow more vibrant at night, lighting up Petaling Street and its surroundings. Chinatown's Petaling Street night market serves as the area's main attraction even bigger and more happening than during the daytime giving you a kind of nightlife that is quite different from what you may be used to.

Located just a two-minute stroll from the Pasar Seni LRT station, Chinatown Kuala Lumpur nightlife is mostly frequented by budget travellers staying in this part of KL, where a couple of watering holes can be found within walking distances from backpacker inns and inexpensive guesthouses. One of the most popular bars in the area is Reggae Bar Chinatown, a groovy and colourful bar that serves a satisfying selection of alcoholic beverages with reggae music being played on constant rotation.

PS150 Bar Kuala Lumpur

PS150 Bar Kuala Lumpur is the first-ever cocktail bar in Chinatown KL, offering an impressive list of Southeast Asian-style cocktails by prominent local mixologist Angel Ng. Occupying a long-abandoned brothel along the back alleyway in Jalan Petaling, this venue is fitted with three distinctive spaces, each of which inspired by different Indochinese eras.

After passing through a deceptively rundown entrance, you'll reach Opium Den, which features private seating booths, bare-bricked walls, and red lanterns, followed by Tiki, an open-air courtyard that can accommodate large crowds. Lastly, the speakeasy-inspired main section is where you'll find a fully-stocked bar that's fitted with an array of repurposed furniture while oriental-style music plays unobtrusively for easy conversation.

PS150 Kuala Lumpur's drinks menu is divided into prominent cocktail eras such as Vintage, Prohibition, Tiki, Disco, and Contemporary. Priced between RM38 and RM230, you can find one signature cocktail and several classic cocktails with an Asian twist in each category. To keep things interesting, there are also new cocktails available every three months.

Standout drinks include the Pandan Flip (RM38), a pandan-infused dark rum with coconut, bitters, and egg yolk and The Last Rite (RM50), which contains gin, Chartreuse, maraschino liquor, absinthe, and lime. If you find standard lychee martinis too sweet for your liking, we highly recommend PS150 Kuala Lumpur's Lychee No. 3 due to its unique blend of London dry gin, lychee, ginger flower, and lime.

Every Sunday between 15:00 and 22:00, the bar hosts a genre-of-the-week event where patrons can provide their music playlist of up to 30 minutes using Spotify, iPod or smartphone. Located in Chinatown KL, PS150 Kuala Lumpur is a five-minute walk from Petaling Street.

PS150 Bar

Opening Hours: Tuesday Saturday 18:00 02:00, Sunday 15:00 22:00
Address: 150 Jalan Petaling, Ground Floor, Chinatown Kuala Lumpur
Tel: +6010 260 6013

Reggae Bar Chinatown in Kuala Lumpur

Reggae Bar Chinatown is exactly what it says it is: a groovy and colourful bar playing reggae music, with photos of Bob Marley and other legends of the genre on the walls. The only bar in the area, it is an ultra friendly place knee-deep in backpackers, set along Jalan Tun HS Lee.

Just down the road is the Reggae Bar Guesthouse, which explains some of its popularity with travellers. Ladies are given especially good prices on drinks. Bob Marley songs seem to be on constant rotation and the place is artfully decked out in red, yellow and green

The Menu
With a tagline 'Love All, Feed All' is it any wonder that the cuisine at Reggae Bar Chinatown is so popular? The

menu consists of mostly western fare with salads, soups, steaks, fish and chips, pizzas, pastas and tapas all featured.

Reggae Bar Changkat

There are two branches of Reggae Bar: the first was established in Chinatown while the second set up shop along Changkat Bukit Bintang years later. They could not be more different, with Reggae Bar Chinatown attracting a young, backpacker crowd and offering cheap drinks, pool tables, Bob Marley hits and some R&B thrown in for good measure.

Reggae Bar Changkat is set at the other end of the spectrum with live music performances and a thoroughly upscale atmosphere. The club features red velvet baroque couches, red carpets, dim lighting and an exclusive atmosphere. Be sure to check out the cool neon-lit staircase that leads up to a more spacious lounge.

Reggae Bar Chinatown
Opening Hours: 12:00 02:00

Location: Across the street from Popular Bookstore
Address: 158, Ground Floor, Jalan Tun H. S. Lee
Tel: +603 2026 7690

Shopping

The Kuala Lumpur shopping scene is a pretty comprehensive one. For high end fashion, the Bukit Bintang and KLCC areas provide the most variety, with upmarket malls such as Pavilion KL and Suria KLCC home to international brands such as Jimmy Choo, Diane Von Fürstenberg and Louis Vuitton. Meanwhile, shopping centres like Low Yat Plaza and Berjaya Times Square are great places to spend your ringgit on tech-related products, and indie fashion finds. We just love street markets too, such as Petaling Street and handicraft emporium Central Market the perfect places to get a real sense of the city's local shopping scene.

There's something for every taste and budget here: designer labels, local indie brands, and street markets with artsy finds and cheap reproductions it all depends on what you are looking for when shopping in Kuala Lumpur…

Bukit Bintang Shopping

The Bukit Bintang shopping scene is home to many designer brands with flagship stores inside popular malls, but there are also affordable department retailers, like Daiso and Debenhams, plus a few local indie labels here too. It goes without saying that shopping in Bukit Bintang is quite a satisfying experience no matter what you are looking for.

Malls like Pavilion KL and Starhill Gallery have high end brands like Louis Vuitton, Jimmy Choo and Coach, while Low Yat Plaza, Sungei Wang Plaza and Berjaya Times Square are perfect for cheap fashion finds and the latest gadgets. We love Fahrenheit 88 which has got the perfect combination of familiar fashion names like Uniqlo and H&M, as well local labels like Area 27, Eclipse and Zang Toi. Plus, the indoor theme park at

Berjaya Times Square is just great fun when you're with the whole family...

Pavilion Shopping Mall in Kuala Lumpur

Pavilion Kuala Lumpur is KL's haute couture shopping Mecca. It takes a lot to stand out in the city's mallscape but this shopping centre, which occupies prime real estate along Jalan Bukit Bintang, does just that. Opened in 2007 it has three major sections a retail mall, an office block and two residential towers.

Keeping the city's fashionistas looking polished, this KL staple is the perfect example of how extravagant some malls can be. It features almost the same staggering square footage as Mid Valley Megamall and 1 Utama and the 1.37 million-sqft white marble complex is a combination of indoor and outdoor shopping venues.

It resembles an oversized Grecian temple with post modern pillars, but instead of torches and an altar with a statue of Zeus, it houses over 450 snazzy stores.

With hip dining options, big-box retailers and access to both international designer labels and local specialty retailers, Pavilion KL is a favourite among KL-ites. Popular no matter the day of the week or time of day, the seven-storey lifestyle centre has six shopping 'zones' and a row of street boutiques.

At the main entrance of Pavilion KL is the tallest Liuli Crystal fountain in Malaysia, the Pavilion Crystal Fountain. Billed as a national landmark, just like Rome's Trevi Fountain you can toss in your loose change to make a wish: coins are later donated to charity.

Opposite Bintang Circle (an open atrium in Pavilion KL used as a promotional space for events) is Singaporean department store Parkson Grand which spans three stories. Other expected, fully stocked anchor shops include Mercato Supermarket and Harvey Norman.

At Pavilion KL Malaysian fashion brands like Jimmy Choo can be found alongside big-ticket European luxury retailers such as Coach, Diane Von Furstenberg, Dolce & Gabbana, Juicy Couture, MaxMara, Versace and Yves Saint Laurent.

High-end browsing takes place at Couture Pavilion where upmarket, international fashion outposts (a majority of them occupying double-storey street front lots) like Michael Kors and Marc by Marc Jacobs are at. Meanwhile inside Pavilion KL are lower-priced, mid-market international and local brands such as Forever 21, Pull & Bear, MNG Mango and Salabianca.

A feature that makes Pavilion KL popular is its all-encompassing holiday décor. For example its 2011 Christmas décor included a Christmas carnival set up in its atrium, complete with Santa's workshop, 10-foot high pine trees, giant sleighs and other baubles and gifts.

Brands found at Pavilion KL

Couture Pavilion
Couture Pavilion is the place to find the latest

collections from international and local high fashion designers.

Bell & Ross	Ermenegildo Zegna	Mikimoto
Bottega Veneta	Giuseppe Zanotti	Montblanc
Bvlgari	Gucci	Prada
Celine	Hermes	Rolex
Chopard	Jimmy Choo	TOD's
Elie Bleu		

Fashion Avenue

Those looking for brands that do not carry such hefty price tags can head to Fashion Avenue where brands like Laura Mercier and Victoria's Secret can be found.

Aesop	Denim & Supply Ralph Lauren	Liuli
Armani Jeans		Victoria's Secret Beauty & Accessories
Bread & Butter	Gordon Max	
Celio	Jo Malone London	
Crabtree &	Laura Mercier	

Evelyn

Tokyo Street

If you are more interested in unique Asian fashion styles, then pay a visit to the new Tokyo Street in Pavilion KL: the brands found here are also reasonably-priced and one-of-a-kind.

Kawaii-Kawaii	Maneki Neiko	The Jekyll & Hyde Project
Kenji Corner	Nike	
Kumo by Leng Yein	Su.Soku	

Food

There is a food court (Gourmet Emporium) on the lower ground floor where you can get reasonably priced Korean, Japanese and local fare. Strategically placed around the food court are upmarket restaurants like Manhattan Fish Market, Dragon-I, Tony Roma's and Madam Kwan's.

Cosmopolites usually dine at Connection, an outdoor strip with restaurants such as Tom, Dick & Harry's Live and The Pressroom Bistro. These places provide entertainment (think live local bands and televised soccer matches on projector screens) and alcohol to go with their meals.

Entertainment

You will not find extreme entertainment options here like Berjaya Times Square's indoor theme park: no, this is the place where you come to spend cash.

Entertainment-wise there is a Red Box karaoke bar where you can belt tunes out at, or if you prefer the lure of the big screen, head on over to the 13-screen Golden Screen Cinemas (GSC). Other than that, the mall's top floors are home to spa outfits and beauty retailers like ADONIS Wellness @ Seventh Heaven and Aster Spring Origin of Beauty.

KL's hot and humid weather make indoor shopping centres wildly popular with the locals, so expect crowds at Pavilion KL especially during the weekend. Pavilion KL can be reached using several public transportation lines: the Bukit Bintang and Raja Chulan monorail stations are just a few minutes walk away.

Whether you are hunting for the latest limited-edition Coach clutch, fresh sushi or if you are simply eager to put your feet and sip on a pint while enjoying the game on the telly, Pavilion KL is the place to be.

Pavilion Kuala Lumpur Shopping Mall
Opening Hours: 10:00 22:00
Location: Right next to Grand Millennium Kuala Lumpur, across the street from JW Marriott and Starhill Gallery.
Address: 168 Jalan Bukit Bintang, 55100
Tel: +603 2118 8833

Starhill Gallery Kuala Lumpur

Starhill Gallery is one of those ritzy shopping malls where you are almost afraid to touch things. Ambient lighting, soft jazz music playing in the background and carpeted floors that mask any sound your feet might make, results in this being a red carpet retail experience like no other.

The hushed atmosphere is exacerbated by smiling, smartly dressed doormen waiting to usher you into stores: coupled with the muted atmosphere, their ever-present presence makes you feel like you have to speak in whispers. You may ask, since Starhill Gallery offers the same haute couture stores all under one roof, as Pavilion KL, what makes it so different? Well, the answer to that is simple Starhill Gallery is an experience, and a decadent one at that.

Developed by the YTL Corporation, Starhill Gallery is the most upscale, luxury retail mall in the prominent Bukit Bintang district. Opened in 1996, it houses more than 100 renowned luxury timepiece and jewellery brands and dozens of other contemporary luxury labels.

The 250,000sqft ritzy retail podium was originally anchored by the Singapore-based Tangs departmental store until it shut down in 2004 due to 'poor financial returns from its expansion abroad'. The mall was renovated in 2005, with renowned American architect David Rockwell at the helm of the project, which resulted in its current glass dome-like façade. At the end of 2010, Starhill Gallery along with its YTL brother, Lot 10 began another bout of renovations and both malls remain open despite these widespread refurbishments.

The main concourse is a spacious open-concept area which plays host to a stage as well as exclusive cafés that surround it. The seven-storey shopping centre has escalators in this area and elevators are located at the back section of the mall beside the well-kept bathrooms.

The first floor of the mall is largely occupied by jewellery and luxury watch brands such as Maurice Lacroix, M Missoni, Korloff, Davidoff, Rado and more; each year Starhill Gallery plays host to Asia's largest luxury watch and jewellery showcase.

Alternatively, if you're looking to relax and unwind in the middle of the day, then the third floor of the mall is home to a 50,000sqft spa and relaxation centre (known as the Pamper Zone) this area has 93 treatment rooms and includes services by some of the best therapists in KL.

The lower ground floor of the plays host to the expansive Feast Village a food court that really isn't your average eatery; the ultra posh food quad plays host to a dozen award-winning restaurants that sport trendy design and fashionable themes. Noteworthy is Fisherman's Cove a makeshift boathouse-like restaurant (set with bamboo furniture, faux sails, masts and nets) that features a fresh seafood menu; booths at the mezzanine floor resemble bamboo sheds. The restaurant has been the recipient of the Best Restaurant award from Time Out and the *Malaysian Tatler* magazine in 2006, 2008 and 2010 respectively.

Meanwhile, Jake's Charbroil Steaks (a branch of the 24-year veteran of the steak-and-seafood industry) is also located in the Feast Village. Featuring an old cowboy town atmosphere with dining booths hewn from 24-year-old Scandinavian pine and Wild West décor, the eatery is an especially popular venture in Starhill Gallery and come dinnertime it's usually crowded.

Additionally, the iconic The Village Bar with stacked glass bottle pillars, colourful pendant lights and clear bar stools, is a must-visit drinking joint; the posh watering hole has five bars dividing its drink selection offering beer, wine, hard liquor, rice wine and soft drinks bars.

Starhill Gallery sits directly adjacent to Pavilion KL and is connected to the five-star JW Marriott Kuala Lumpur hotel. Cosmetics behemoth Sephora is located beside it and just down the road is the sister venture of Pavilion KL, the newly-opened Fahrenheit 88. Starhill Gallery faces Jalan Gading and Jalan Bukit Bintang and is also linked to the Ritz-Carlton Hotel by a sky bridge.

Starhill Gallery

Highlights: Shook! Restaurant, Porsche Design, Fendi, Asprey, Louis Vuitton, Omega, Givenchy, Dior, Tag Heuer, Lacoste, Royal Selangor, Jogoya Japanese Restaurant.
Opening Hours: Daily, 10:00 22:00
Location: Across the street from Pavilion KL, right next to Fahrenheit.
Address: 181, Jalan Bukit Bintang, 55100 Kuala Lumpur
Tel: +603 2782 3855

Low Yat Plaza Shopping Mall

Low Yat Plaza commonly referred to as LYP or Low Yat is a well established commercial shopping centre in Kuala Lumpur's busy city centre. Specializing in electronics and IT products, it's located directly opposite the popular Berjaya Times Square shopping mall. Ranking high as one of the city's best known spots for gadgets and gizmos, the 12-storey mall is divided into a series of inter-connected stores surrounding a main concourse.

History

In 2006, the Ministry of Domestic Trade and Consumer Affairs raided Loy Yat Plaza and Imbi Plaza and confiscated more than 27,000 copies of pirated computer software and movies. Since then, the complex has shaken off its less-than-savoury reputation and transformed into a respectable business location, reclaiming its spot as the city's pre-eminent IT mall

Store Structure

The Malaysian equivalent of Singapore's Sim Lim Square and Funan, the complex is sandwiched between Sungei Wang Plaza and Melia Hotel Kuala Lumpur, just off Jalan Bukit Bintang. Its main competitor is Imbi Plaza, an older IT mall.

Escalators run through the centre of the complex and each floor within the mall is dedicated to stores occupying retail spaces that range from small-time ventures to large-scale shop lots. Toshiba, Nokia, Celcom, Sony, Digi, Microsoft, Dell, Maxis, Fotokem,

HTC, Samsung, Nikon, Acer and Lenovo are just a few stores that occupy retail space here.

With so many specialty shops, you'll find that the merchandise found in the mall, including electronic parts, are competitively-priced and prices are usually negotiable. Some stores even offer computer-related services and friendly staff are more than happy to fix your gadgets while bypassing the technical jargon. These tech experts assemble computer parts, install computer software and fix mobile phones and cameras for a nominal charge.

Food and Entertainment

There are various eateries scattered throughout the gadget-savvy complex the basement level plays host to a branch of the popular Red Box karaoke bar. Meanwhile, the lower ground floors houses a food court which serves a variety of local specialties, Korean and Japanese favourites and audio and video-related stores; there's also a branch of the popular Old Town kopitiam on this level.

The ground floor of the shopping podium sees the most pedestrian traffic stores are positioned around a main courtyard and display cases are placed haphazardly outside the front doors of each store. Restaurants such as Sushi King, Big Apple Doughnuts and Hainan Tea which serves local favourites such as nasi lemak have set up shop here. There are also camera, laptop and cell phone stores as well as a Guardian pharmacy; meanwhile, the upper ground floor houses games and camera stores as well as a café.

The first floor is where you can purchase cell phone accessories; there are also a variety of clothes boutiques and a bookstore. The mall's anchor tenant IT Computes Centre occupies the second, third and fourth floors.

Technical Info

The mall's range of facilities is adequate there are large retail podium restrooms and ATM machines (beside the Coffee Bean & Tea Leaf Café) throughout the complex. Nearby public transportation access is plentiful as the Bukit Bintang and Imbi Monorail stations are merely a short walk away.

Low Yat Plaza
Highlights: Red Box Karaoke, TecAsia, Bee Connection, All I.T. Hypermarket, Hewlett-Packard, Sony Centre.
Opening Hours: Daily, 10:00 22:00
Location: Behind Amoda Building, which is across the street from Berjaya Times Square, and right beside Bukit Bintang Plaza/Sungei Wang Plaza.
Address: No. 7 Jalan Bintang, Off Jalan Bukit Bintang, Bukit Bintang Central, 55100 Kuala Lumpur.
Malaysia.
Tel: +603 2148 3651

Kuala Lumpur Chinatown Shopping

Shopping in Kuala Lumpur Chinatown is a must when visiting this big, bustling city. Spread across several streets including Jalan Petaling, Jalan Tun Tan Cheng Lock and Jalan Hang Kasturi, Chinatown's shopping bargains are deals of a lifetime, especially at the Petaling Street Night Market. What's more, shopping in Chinatown is not just about buying modern items; a lot of locals visiting the herbal shops are here to purchase traditional medicine.

Without a doubt, Jalan Petaling, or Petaling Street as locals call it, is the most popular. Housed under a green glass roof, which allows the daily market to operate all day, it is crammed with market stalls selling reproduction designer handbags, shoes, apparel and more. Central Market KL is not too far away either and remains a favourite Kuala Lumpur Chinatown shopping spot for its one-of-a-kind local artwork and souvenirs.

Kasturi Walk in Kuala Lumpur

Kasturi Walk is a covered, open-air flea market set along Jalan Kasturi, a lane running alongside Central Market. Here, you'll find local snacks and vendors selling fake label handbags, watches, T-shirts, flip flops and more as well as fruit stalls. It is similar to Petaling Street but not as crowded.

Right over the front entrance of the tiled walkway is a pewter wau bulan (a type of Malay kite) which looks like a butterfly. Although Kasturi Walk does not have the same extensive range of traders as Petaling Street the goods are reasonably priced plus its convenient location makes a trip here worthwhile. It was established in early 2011, so it all looks fairly new with clean kiosks and stalls.

Food stalls sell everything from Malay kuih and Chinese dim sum to Indian rojak and other local snacks. A popular spot with tourists, during special events Kasturi Walk organises cultural performances. Sometimes you can get even better bargains at Kasturi Walk than at Central Market.

To get there using the LRT, alight at the Pasir Seni station: from there it is only a few minutes walk to Kasturi Walk; the KTM Komuter also has a stop (Kuala Lumpur) nearby the market. Another easy way is to hop on a bus or taxi; nearby landmarks include Petaling Street, the Dayabumi Complex and National Mosque.

Kasturi Walk

Highlights: local snacks and vendors selling fake label handbags, watches, T-shirts, flip flops and more as well as fruit stalls. Read more: Kuala Lumpur Chinatown Shopping - Where to Shop and What to Buy in Chinatown http://www.kuala-lumpur.ws/klareas/chinatown_shopping.htm#ixzz1n5wHrQgM
Opening Hours: 10:00 21:30
Location: Jalan Kasturi

Petaling Street in Chinatown

Ask anyone who's been to Malaysia about Petaling Street and they will cite it as a shopper's haven, albeit in a different league when compared to its more glamourous counterparts, Bukit Bintang and KLCC. A well-known shopping district, the whole area transforms into a lively and vibrant night market after dark, with hundreds of stalls selling all kinds of stuff at dirt-cheap prices, making it the most happening night market in the city.

Petaling Street Historical Background

Back in the olden days when Malaysia was still known as 'Tanah Melayu' or Malaya, the Chinese had come to this country to work at the tin mines. However, during the Selangor Civil War, the tin mines were temporarily abandoned. The Chinese returned after the war, only to find the mines flooded. Yap Ah Loy, an influential Chinese figure back then, had opened a tapioca mill on Petaling Street in his bid to persuade the Chinese to stay on. To this day, Petaling Street is sometimes called 'Chee Cheong Kai', meaning 'Starch Factory Street' in Cantonese, referring to its history as the centre for the production of tapioca flour back then.

Since then, Petaling Street has been given a facelift. Gone are the patchy roads, broken pavements and colourful umbrellas attached to wooden pushcarts lining the street on both sides. A green awning covers the length of the street, acting as a roof to shield vendors and shoppers from the heat and the rain. An Oriental-style archway with the words 'Jalan Petaling/Petaling Street' spelled out in gold letters greets visitors at its main entrance.

Shopper's Haven & Foodie's Galore

Petaling Street is chock-full of shops and stalls selling goods and food. A signboard warning against the sale of imitation goods provides an interesting even ironic contrast as the whole street is practically littered with fake branded items. Handbags, watches, trainers, clothing you name it, they've got it. Louis Vuitton sits side-by-side with Rolex, and you can sometimes get the latest cinematic releases at less than RM 10 each. For shoppers on a tight budget or those looking for cheap and cheerful 'branded' goods, Petaling Street will be their first stop as it offers not just variety but also value for money as the prices can be further whittled down through hard bargaining.

Petaling Street is also filled with opportunities to sample a delightful array of local cuisine. Chinese and seafood restaurants can be found at every corner, and stalls selling all kinds of snacks are stretched along the street, resulting in an interesting mixture of aroma filling the air that is quite hard to resist. The best thing about them is that most of them are open until very late at night, with some even staying open until four to five in the morning. For a highly-recommended list of food to try in and around Petaling Street, take a look at our Chinatown Dining section.

Bargaining Tips
Bargaining is the way to go when shopping in Petaling Street, unless you don't mind being ripped off. Prices are generally quoted 15 to 35% higher than what they are truly worth even higher sometimes for tourists. So before you head down to Petaling Street, make sure your bargaining skills are well-honed.

But first things first before going on your haggling venture, pay attention to what you're wearing. If you look like you have the money, some vendors will not hesitate to charge you double or even triple the price. So leave your Armani shirt and gold wristwatch behind, and dress as simply as you could. Wear no visible labels or anything that is a dead giveaway to your financial status.

When you find an item you like, take your time to inspect it. Keep a neutral expression and don't let your interest show too much, even if you're dead keen on it. Even if there's a price tag on the item clearly stating what it's worth, still make it a point to ask: "How much?" The bidding process will thus begin. Start with offering just one quarter of the asking price don't feel bad about this as you can always raise your offer bit by bit.

Keep going back and forth with your counter-offer until you reach a price that you're comfortable with. If the vendor refuse to budge any lower, thank him, tell him that you will think about it and walk away to survey other shops. Two things will happen: 1) the vendor calls you back and states his final (and much lower) offer or asks you how much you're willing to pay for the item, or 2) you will find a much better offer elsewhere. The mistake that most foreigners make is that they're too afraid, too embarrassed or feel too guilty to ask for a much lower price, that they immediately accept the first counter-offer that the vendor makes. Remember, most of the items sold here initially bear a higher marked price, so don't be afraid to bid lower, and feel free to shop around it is the culture here

Getting to Petaling Street
Chinatown is served by a good network of public transportation. Major bus routes operate through this area just take the ones heading for 'Kotaraya'. There are also plenty of train stations nearby; you can either take the LRT (Pasar Seni or Masjid Jamek station), KTM Komuter (Kuala Lumpur station) or Monorail (Maharajalela station) all within walking distance

Hotels

Kuala Lumpur hotels can really adapt to all budgets, from famous five-star hotel brands, to fun boutique hotels with cool and quirky designs, and, of course, some very affordable accommodation for budget travellers. We have compiled here a great collection of the best hotels in Kuala Lumpur at great rates, all sorted into different style and location categories to simplify your search for the right Kuala Lumpur hotel.

Without a doubt the most popular area to stay when you're visiting Kuala Lumpur is Bukit Bintang - a locale closest to some of KL's best bars and nightclubs. If you prefer staying close to the city's iconic landmarks, KLCC and Chinatown KL are your best bets as both districsts host a wide range of accomodation options that are within walking distance to ornate temples, sleek skyscrapers, and historical architecture. To help you get started on your holiday in the capital city of Malaysia

The 10 best centrally located hotels in Kuala Lumpur serve as great jumping off points to explore the city's top tourist sites, including the iconic Petronas Twin Towers and Menara KL. Ranging from luxury hotel franchises to frills-free but sophisticated accommodation options, they gather acclaim not only for their great locations in the heart of KL, but also for their top notch service.

Wine and dine at some of the city's best restaurants, clubs and bars within walking distance, or get some much-needed shopping done at nearby malls like Pavilion KL or Low Yat Plaza. Meanwhile, families with little ones will love the fact that there is so much to do within the city centre. The options on our list of the most popular centrally located hotels in Kuala Lumpur are within walking distance to some pretty fun attractions such as the indoor theme park at Berjaya Times Square and indoor oceanarium at Suria KLCC

Mandarin Oriental Kuala Lumpur

With a stay at Mandarin Oriental Kuala Lumpur, you'll be centrally located in Kuala Lumpur, just a 5-minute walk from Petronas Twin Towers and 12 minutes by foot from Suria KLCC Shopping Centre.Featured amenities include a business center, limo/town car service, and express check-in.Event facilities at this hotel consist of conference space and meeting rooms.Free self parking is available onsite.

Shangri-La Hotel - Kuala Lumpur
Shangri-La Hotel Kuala Lumpurs sidewalk is shaded by a leafy canopy of green trees and once you are inside, it is evident why this is one of the citys most popular hotels: rich, inviting and warm are words that perfectly sum up its interior design.Subtle local touches are imbued into almost every aspect - from staff members scarlet and gold uniforms, traditional songket kebayas to the Malaysian greeting (a hand over the heart and a slight bow) that greets you at every turn.The pool has such a stunning close-up view of the PETRONAS Twin Towers that it almost feels like it is slotted in between the two blocks.

Oasia Suites Kuala Lumpur
With a stay at Oasia Suites Kuala Lumpur, you'll be centrally located in Kuala Lumpur, within a 5-minute drive of Kuala Lumpur Tower and Pavilion Kuala Lumpur.Featured amenities include dry

cleaning/laundry services, a 24-hour front desk, and luggage storage. Free self parking is available onsite.

Renaissance Hotel KL
If easy access is your number one priority, Renaissance Kuala Lumpur Hotel should be on top of your list. Within walking distance to the Monorail Bukit Nenas and LRT Dang Wangi, it takes up prime territory on the corner of Jalan Ampang and Jalan Sultan Ismail. The hotel is surrounded by popular city attractions including KL Tower and Suria KLCC. It is also designed with convenience in mind - a fully-equipped gym complete with personal trainers, a Balinese-inspired spa, and award-winning on-site restaurants are all on the menu!. The hotel carries two distinct themes - the West Wing rooms are influenced by classic European style with heavy dark wood furniture, sunshine yellow walls and lots of chocolate accents.

Concorde Hotel KL
Practically an institution in Kuala Lumpur, Concorde Hotel has stood the test of time and is still a great

choice for both business and leisure travellers who wants great value accommodation while being in the middle of the action.Its location is Jalan Sultan Ismail, which means its within walking distance to both Petronas Twin Towers and KL Tower, together with Asian Heritage Row (a nightlife spot) and Monorail Bukit Nenas station, so you can easily hop on and discover more of the city.Live music options are plentiful at Concorde, with the well-known Hard Rock Cafe right next door of the hotel, and onsite classy Western restaurant Spices featuring a live pianist playing from 20:00.

Hotel Maya Kuala Lumpur
Ticking all the right boxes, we just cannot sing Hotel Mayas praises enough - first lets talk about its excellent location - just opposite the five-star property is super nightclub, Zouk KL, while just around the corner (a five-minute walk) is Suria KLCC.Stylish and chic, hotel amenities include a business centre with secretarial services, ballroom, six meeting rooms and five F&B

venues. We especially love Sky Lounge, a bistro reserved exclusively for hotel guests, where you can enjoy complimentary drinks and snacks from 21:00 - 23:00. Leisure facilities include an on-site spa (with six treatment rooms), an amazing hydrotherapy pool and a gym with scheduled yoga and Pilates classes.

Grand Hyatt Kuala Lumpur
For those who appreciate the finer things in life, look no further than Grand Hyatt Kuala Lumpur as your accommodation while in the city. Occupying a spot in the Golden Triangle, it is within walking distance to well-known city landmarks: Petronas Twin Towers, Kuala Lumpur Convention Centre and KLCC Park are all close by and Pavilion KL is connected via a covered sky-bridge outside the hotel. You can count on the Hyatt brand for a complete range of facilities, including a 24-hour fitness centre that is well-equipped with personal trainers, LCD screens and internet access, and the Essa Spa, fitted with 11 treatment rooms, Jacuzzi, steam, sauna and ice fountain rooms.

Traders Hotel KL

Traders Hotel Kuala Lumpur by Shangri-La is a five-star hotel located opposite Suria KLCC - with the Petronas Twin Towers and Kuala Lumpur Convention Centre flanking it. With an unbeatable location and business amenities such as free Wi-Fi, a business centre with secretarial service and five on-site meeting rooms, it is the perfect hotel for business and a great place to stay if you want to be in the thick of things. Leisure facilities are impressive - right in front of the 34-storey hotel is the KLCC Park, which hosts a 1.3km jogging track. Besides that the hotel has a pool, fully-equipped gym with sauna, a spa with five treatment rooms and three F&B venues (including Sky Bar, one of the citys premier rooftop bars).

Grand Millennium KL

Glitzy and glamorous, Grand Millennium Kuala Lumpur is the perfect stay for those who are looking for convenience in terms of location and accommodation. Boasting 468 guestrooms and suites, the hotel stands in a prime location of Bukit Bintang C its neighbours are the shopping malls Pavilion, Starhill and Fahrenheit 88, and it is within walking distance of the Bukit Bintang Monorail station so getting to other attractions within the city is a breeze. The hotel exudes an aura of exclusivity but maintains tranquility, no more so than in its black-and-gold themed lobby. Rooms are spacious and come complete with amenities such as LCD flat-screen TVs with satellite channels and broadband internet access.

The Ritz-Carlton, Kuala Lumpur
With a stay at The Ritz-Carlton, Kuala Lumpur, you'll be centrally located in Kuala Lumpur, within a 10-minute drive of Petronas Twin Towers and Suria KLCC Shopping Centre. Featured amenities include a business center, limo/town car service, and dry cleaning/laundry services. Limited parking is available onsite.

The End

www.ingramcontent.com/pod-product-compliance
Lightning Source LLC
Chambersburg PA
CBHW031102080526
44587CB00011B/782